Table of Contents

INTRODUCTION TO DAY TRADING

Welcome to the first part of your Day Trading learning experience. In the following articles, you will learn the core concepts of day trading, what resources you must have at your disposal, and whether your personality traits are suitable for day trading. We will also discuss the topics of money management, backtesting day trading strategies via appropriate software, and using demo accounts to recover enough smoothed statistical data.

The section will also cover several methods of evaluating a strategy performance based on gathered historical data, as well as determining the most important long-term and short-term factors driving the Foreign Exchange market. Let us begin !,

There was once a time when the only people who were able to trade actively in the stock market were those working for large financial institutions, brokerages, and trading houses. But, with the rise of the internet and online trading houses, brokers have made it easier for the average individual investor to get in on the game.

Day trading can turn out to be a very lucrative career, as long as you do it properly. But it can also be a little challenging for novices—especially for those who aren't fully prepared with a well-planned strategy. Even the most seasoned day traders can hit rough patches and experience losses. So, what exactly is day trading and how does it work?

Day Trading Defined

Day trading is the activity of buying and selling financial instruments (stocks, bonds, options, futures, or commodities) with the intent of profiting from price movements in the underlying security within a single trading day. While positions may be held for seconds to hours during the day, they are always closed out before the market close to avoid overnight exposure risk. Entering a position (also known as opening a position) and then exiting the same position (also known as closing the position) is defined as a round trip. For example, buying 100 shares of XYZ stock at $26 and selling 100 shares of XYZ stock $26.30 approximately 20 minutes later. Day trading is a series of speculative round trips executed inside of market hours. Swing trading allows for holding positions overnight to several days.

Since the technology bubble, the markets have become more efficient with computerization, as auction pits have been replaced with computer screens. Retail broker platforms and tools have advanced to allow day traders to analyze technical and fundamental information with a few keystrokes. While fraction-based price spreads have been replaced with decimal-based penny increments, the commission structure has also been improved. Access to news and information combined with instant fills and order modifications have produced more sophisticated day traders. Algorithm and high-frequency trading programs control up to 70% of the market movements. This has provided opportunities for day traders that can take advantage of the price action.

Traders should always know when they plan to enter or exit a trade before they execute. By using stop losses effectively, a trader can minimize not only losses but also the number of times a trade is exited needlessly. Make your battle plan ahead of time so you'll already know you've won the war. Overall investor sentiment frequently drives market performance in directions that are at odds with the fundamentals. The successful investor controls fear and greed, the two human emotions that drive that sentiment. Understanding this can give you the discipline and objectivity needed to take advantage of others' emotions.

Aspiring traders should beware of websites and courses that promise foolproof day trading success or endless profits. The limited percentage of day traders who have managed to be successful do so by investing their time and efforts into building trading strategies and following them religiously. A day trader is on his own in this big trading world. Before giving up your job to become a day trader, be sure that you have the motivation to continuously learn, design your trading strategies, and take accountability for your decisions and actions. If you're looking to jump into the world of day trading, you can use one of the best stock brokers for day trading.

Having a plan is essential for achieving trading success. A trading plan should be written in stone, but is subject to reevaluation and can be adjusted along with changing market conditions. A solid trading plan considers the trader's style and goals. Knowing when to exit a trade is just as important as knowing when to enter the position. Stop-loss prices and profit targets should be added to the trading plan to identify specific exit points for each trade.

CHAPTER 1 - HOW DAY TRADING WORKS

Day trading is speculation in securities, specifically buying and selling financial instruments within the same trading day, such that all positions are closed before the market closes for the trading day. Traders who trade in this capacity with the motive of profit are therefore speculators. The methods of quick trading contrast with the long-term trades underlying buy and hold and value investing strategies. Day traders exit positions before the market close to avoid unmanageable risks and negative price gaps between one day's close and the next day's price at the open.

The Basics Of Day Trading

Day trading is defined as the purchase and sale of a security within a single trading day. It can occur in any marketplace but is most common in the foreign exchange (forex) and stock markets.

Day traders are typically well-educated and well-funded. They use high amounts of leverage and short-term trading strategies to capitalize on small price movements in highly liquid stocks or currencies.

Day traders are attuned to events that cause short-term market moves. Trading the news is a popular technique. Scheduled announcements such as economic statistics, corporate earnings, or interest rates are subject to market expectations and market psychology. Markets react when those expectations are not met or are exceeded, usually with sudden, significant moves, which can benefit day traders.

What Is Day Trading?

The definition of "day trading" is the buying and selling of a security in a single trading day. If you're day trading online you will close out your position before the markets close for the day to secure your profits. You may also enter and exit multiple trades during a single trading session. Day trading is the practice of buying and selling stocks in a short timeframe, typically a day. The goal is to earn a tiny profit on each trade and then compound those gains over time.

With the rise of online stock brokers and cheap trades, day trading became a viable (albeit very risky) way for retail investors to turn a few days' worths of quick wins into a substantial bankroll. Brokers on occasion have different definitions for 'active' or day traders. Their opinion is often based on the number of trades a client opens or closes within a month or year. Some brands even refer to 'hyper-active traders' – a step beyond the 'active trader'.

Day trading is normally done by using trading strategies to capitalize on small price movements in high-liquidity stocks or currencies. The purpose of DayTrading.com is to give you an overview of day trading basics and what it takes for you to make it as a day trader. From scalping a few pips profit in minutes on a forex trade to trading news events on stocks or indices – we explain how.

Equipment And Software For Day Trading Beginners

You Need A Few Basic Tools To Day Trade:

Computer Or Laptop

Having two monitors is preferable, but not required. The computer should have enough memory and a fast enough processor that when you run your trading program (discussed later) there is no lagging or crashes. You don't need a top-of-the-line computer, but you don't want to cheap out either. Software and computers are constantly changing, so make sure your computer is keeping up with the times. A slow computer can be costly when day trading, especially if it crashes while you are in trades or its slowness causes you to get stuck in trades.

Reliable, Quick Internet Connection

Day trading isn't recommended with a sporadic internet connection. You should be using at least a cable or ADSL-type internet connection. Speeds vary across these types of services, so strive for at least a mid-range internet package. The slowest speed offered by your internet provider may do the job, but if you have multiple web pages and applications running, then you may notice your trading platform isn't updating as quickly as it should. If your internet goes down a lot, see if there is a more reliable provider.

A Trading Platform

Download several trading platforms and try them out. Since you are a beginner, you won't have a well-developed trading style yet, so just try a few that your broker offers and see which you like best. Keep in mind you may change your trading platform more than once within your career, or you may alter how it is set up to accommodate your trading progress. NinjaTrader is a popular day trading platform for futures and forex traders. There are loads of stock trading platforms.

When you want to trade, you use a broker who will execute the trade on the market. The broker you choose is an important investment decision. Below are some points to look at when picking one:

1. Speed Of Execution: Due to the high number of trades you might make in a day, speed of execution is important – as is getting the price you need, when you need it.

2. Costs: The lower the fees and commission rates, the more viable day trading is. Active traders will be trading often – minimizing these trading costs it vital

3. Regulatory Compliance: Make sure your broker is regulated. They will be legally obliged to protect your financial interests.

4. Support: Whatever your day trading strategy, you'll probably need assistance at some point, so look for online brokers with quick response times and strong customer support.

5. Spreads, Leverage & Margin: As a day trader you want competitive spreads you might also want certain leverage levels and low margins.

6. Trading Platforms: Does it suit your needs? From a stop loss to limit order and advanced charting, the trading platform needs to deliver the tools and features you want.

7. Assets and Markets: A forex trader wants to trade different assets than someone stock trading. Brokers cater to different markets so you need to know you can trade the correct currency pairs or stocks and equities.

Day Trading Strategies

Taking the first momentum examples they see and losing money left, right, and center. Savvy traders will employ day trading strategies in forex, grain futures, and anything else they're trading in, to give them an edge over the market. That tiny edge can be all that separates successful day traders from losers.

There are several day trading techniques and strategies out there, but all will rely on accurate data, carefully laid out in charts and spreadsheets. Options include:

- ❖ Swing trading
- ❖ Scalping
- ❖ Trading zones
- ❖ Trading on volume
- ❖ Arbitrage trading
- ❖ A simple day trading exit strategy
- ❖ Utilizing news

It is those who stick religiously to their short term trading strategies, rules, and parameters that yield the best results. Too many minor losses add up over time.

Characteristics Of A Day Trader

Professional day traders those who trade for a living rather than as a hobby are typically well-established in the field. They usually have in-depth knowledge of the marketplace, too. Here are some of the prerequisites required to be a successful day trader:

Knowledge And Experience In The Marketplace

Individuals who attempt to day trade without an understanding of market fundamentals often lose money. Technical analysis and chart reading is a good skill for a day trader to have, but without a more in-depth understanding of the market you're in and the assets that exist in that market, charts may be deceiving. Do your due diligence and understand the particular ins and outs of the products you trade.

Sufficient Capital

Day traders use only risk capital which they can afford to lose. Not only does this protect them from financial ruin, but it also helps eliminate emotion from their trading. A large amount of capital is often necessary to capitalize effectively on intraday price movements. Having access to a margin account is also key since volatile swings can incur margin calls on short notice.

Strategy

A trader needs an edge over the rest of the market. There are several different strategies day traders use including swing trading, arbitrage, and trading news. These strategies are refined until they produce consistent profits and effectively limit losses.

STRATEGY BREAKDOWN		
TYPE	RISK	REWARD
Swing Trading	High	High
Arbitrage	Low	Medium
Trading News	Medium	Medium
Mergers/Acquisitions	Medium	High

Discipline

A profitable strategy is useless without discipline. Many day traders end up losing a lot of money because they fail to make trades that meet their criteria. As they say, "Plan the trade and trade the plan." Success is impossible without discipline.

To profit, day traders rely heavily on volatility in the market. A stock may be attractive to a day trader if it moves a lot during the day. That could happen because of several different things including an earnings report, investor sentiment, or even general economic or company news. Day traders also like stocks that are heavily liquid because that gives them the chance to change their position without altering the price of the stock. If a stock price moves higher, traders may take a buy position. If the price moves down, a trader may decide to short-sell so he can profit when it falls. Regardless of what technique a day trader uses, they're usually looking to trade a stock that moves... a lot.

Day Trading For A Living

There are two primary divisions of professional day traders: those who work alone and/or those who work for a larger institution. Most day traders who trade for a living work for a large institution. These traders have an advantage because they have access to a direct line, a trading desk, large amounts of capital and leverage, expensive analytical software, and much more. These traders are typically looking for easy profits that can be made from arbitrage opportunities and news events, and these resources allow them to capitalize on these less risky day trades before individual traders can react.

Individual traders often manage other people's money or simply trade with their own. Few of them have access to a trading desk, but they often have strong ties to a brokerage (due to the large amounts they spend on commissions) and access to other resources. However, the limited scope of these resources prevents them from competing directly with institutional day traders. Instead, they are forced to take more risks. Individual traders typically day trade using technical analysis and swing trades combined with some leverage to generate adequate profits on such small price movements in highly liquid stocks.

Day Trading For A Living

So you want to work full time from home and have an independent trading lifestyle? If so, you should know that turning part time trading into a profitable job with a liveable salary requires specialist tools and equipment to give you the necessary edge. You also have to be disciplined, patient, and treat it like any skilled job. Being your boss and deciding your work hours are great rewards if you succeed.

Psychology

If you're trading as a career you have to master your emotions. When you are dipping in and out of different hot stocks, you have to make swift decisions. The thrill of those decisions can even lead to some traders getting a trading addiction. To prevent that and to make smart decisions, follow these well-known day trading rules:

1. Controlling Fear: Even the supposedly best stocks can start plummeting. Fear then sets in and many investors liquidate their holdings. Now whilst they prevent losses, they also wave goodbye to potential gains. Recognizing that fear is a natural reaction will allow you to maintain focus and react rationally.

2. 'Pigs get slaughtered': When you're in a winning position, knowing when to get out before you get whipsawed or blown out of your position isn't easy. Tackling your greed is a hurdle, but one you must overcome. Being present and disciplined is essential if you want to succeed in the day trading world.

Recognizing your psychological pitfalls and separating your emotions is imperative.

Education

DayTrading.com exists because we could not find a reliable day trading school, university, academy, or institute that runs classes where you can get an all-inclusive day trading education. This site should be your main guide when learning how to day trade, but of course, there are other resources out there to complement the material:

- ❖ Podcasts
- ❖ Blogs
- ❖ Online day trading courses
- ❖ Practice game apps
- ❖ Books
- ❖ Ebooks
- ❖ Audiobooks
- ❖ Seminars
- ❖ Journals
- ❖ Message boards like Discord
- ❖ Forums
- ❖ Chat rooms (always free)
- ❖ Newsletters
- ❖ Pdf guides

For the right amount of money, you could even get your very own day trading mentor, who will be there to coach you every step of the way. Opt for the learning tools that best suit your individual needs, and remember, knowledge is power.

Secrets To Success

Whether you're looking for jobs you can do from home, or you want to start day trading as a hobby, follow these seven essentials.

1. Setting Up

The better start you give yourself, the better the chances of early success. That means when you're sat at your desk, staring at your monitors with hands dancing across your keyboard, you're looking at the best sources of information. That means having the best trading platform for your Mac or PC laptop/desktop, having a fast and reliable asset scanner and live stream, and software that won't crash at a pivotal moment.

2. Keep It Simple

This is especially important at the beginning. You might be interested in s&p 500, mutual funds, bond futures, Nasdaq, Nasdaq futures, blue-chip stocks, equities, or the Dax 30, but to start with a focus on only one. Get good at making money from one market/security before you branch out. The other markets will wait for you.

3. Be Realistic

The movies may have made it look easy, but don't be fooled. Even the day trading gurus in college put in the hours. You won't be invited to join that hedge fund after reading just one Bitcoin guide. You need to order those trading books from Amazon, download that spy pdf guide, and learn how it all works.

4. Risk Management

This is one of the most important lessons you can learn. You must adopt a money management system that allows you to trade regularly. Is day trading worth it if you'll be broke by the end of the first month?

History has shown that many successful traders never risk more than 1% of their account balance on a single trade. So, if you had $25000 in your account, you'd only risk $250 on a single trade. Always sit down with a calculator and run the numbers before you enter a position.

5. Keep A Record

One of the day trading fundamentals is to keep a tracking spreadsheet with detailed earnings reports. If you can quickly look back and see where you went wrong, you can identify gaps and address any pitfalls, minimizing losses next time.

6. Timing

Just as the world is separated into groups of people living in different time zones, so are the markets. If you start trading on the Cac 40 at 11:00 ET, you might find you've missed the best entry signals of the day already, minimizing your potential end of day profit. So, if you want to be at the top, you may have to seriously adjust your working hours.

7. Sensible Decision Making

When you start day trading you'll have a host of difficult decisions to make. Should you be using Robinhood? What about day trading on Coinbase? Do you have the right desk setup? Where can you find an excel template? How do you set up a watch list? The meaning of all these questions and much more is explained in detail across the comprehensive pages on this website.

Day trading demands access to some of the most complex financial services and instruments in the marketplace. Day traders typically require:

Access To A Trading Desk

This is usually reserved for traders working for larger institutions or those who manage large amounts of money. The dealing desk provides these traders with instantaneous order executions, which are particularly important when sharp price movements occur. For example, when an acquisition is announced, day traders looking at merger arbitrage can place their orders before the rest of the market can take advantage of the price differential.

Multiple News Sources

News provides the majority of opportunities from which day traders capitalize, so it is imperative to be the first to know when something significant happens. The typical trading room contains access to the Dow Jones Newswire, constant coverage of CNBC and other news organizations, and software that constantly analyzes news sources for important stories.

Analytical Software

Trading software is an expensive necessity for most day traders. Those who rely on technical indicators or swing trades rely more on software than news. This software may be characterized by the following:

1. **Automatic Pattern Recognition:** This means the trading program identifies technical indicators like flags and channels, or more complex indicators such as Elliott Wave patterns.

2. **Genetic And Neural Applications:** These are programs that use neural networks and genetic algorithms to perfect trading systems to make more accurate predictions of future price movements.

3. Broker Integration: Some of these applications even interface directly with the brokerage which allows for an instantaneous and even automatic execution of trades. This helps eliminate emotion from trading and improve execution times.

4. Backtesting: This allows traders to look at how a certain strategy would have performed in the past to predict more accurately how it will perform in the future. Keep in mind that past performance is not always indicative of future results.

Combined, these tools provide traders with an edge over the rest of the marketplace. It is easy to see why, without them, so many inexperienced traders lose money. Additionally, other elements that influence a day trader's earnings potential the market they trade in, how much capital they have, and the time they are willing to devote.

Should You Start Day Trading?

As mentioned above, day trading as a career can be very difficult and quite a challenge. First, you need to come in with some knowledge of the trading world and have a good idea of your risk tolerance, capital, and goals.

1. Day trading is also a career that requires a lot of time. If you want to perfect your strategies after you've practiced, of course and make money, you'll have to devote a lot of time to it. This isn't

something you can do part-time or whenever you get the urge. You have to be fully invested in it.

2. If you do decide that the thrill of trading is right for you, remember to start small. Focus on a few stocks rather than going into the market head-first and wearing yourself thin. Going all out will only complicate your trading strategy and can mean big losses.

3. Finally, stay cool and try to keep the emotion out of your trades. The more you can do that, the more you'll be able to stick to your plan. Keeping a level head allows you to maintain your focus while keeping you on the path you've selected to go down.

If you follow these simple guidelines, you may be headed for a good career in day trading.

How Day Trading Works

Volatility is the name of the day-trading game. Day traders rely heavily on a stock's or market's fluctuations to earn their profits. They like stocks that bounce around a lot throughout the day, whatever the cause: a good or bad earnings report, positive or negative news, or just general market sentiment. They also like highly liquid stocks, ones that allow them to move in and out of a position without much affecting the stock's price.

Day traders might buy a stock if it's moving higher or short-sell it if it's moving lower, trying to profit on a stock's fall. They might trade the same stock many times in a day, buying it one time and then short-selling it the next, taking advantage of changing sentiment. Whichever strategy they use, they're looking for a stock to move.

Why Is Day Trading Hard?

There Are Two Major Reasons:

1. Retail day traders are competing with professionals. Pros know the tricks and traps. They have expensive trading technology, data subscriptions, and personal connections. They're perfectly outfitted to succeed, and even then they often fail. Among these pros are high-frequency traders, who are looking to skim pennies or fractions of pennies the day trader's profit off every trade. It's a crowded field, and the pros love to have inexperienced investors join the fray. That helps them profit.

2. Retail investors are prone to psychological biases that make day trading difficult. They tend to sell winners too early and hold losers too long, what some call "picking the flowers and watering the weeds." That's easy to do when you get a shot of adrenaline for closing out a profitable trade. Investors engage in myopic loss aversion, which renders them too afraid to buy when a stock declines because they fear it might fall further.

Picking A Day Trading Market

All markets offer profit potential. Therefore it often comes down to how much capital you need to get started. Don't try to master all markets at once. This will divide your attention, and it may take longer to make money. Pick one market so that you can focus on your learning. Once you learn to make money in one market, it is easier to adapt to learn other markets. So, be patient. You may already have a market in mind, but here's the background in a nutshell. It comes down to what you like, but also what you can afford.

1. The foreign exchange market, where you're trading currencies such as the euro and U.S. dollar (EUR/USD), requires the least capital. You can get started with as little as $50, although starting with more is recommended.

2. Trading certain futures markets may only require $1,000 to get started. There is also a wide assortment of futures available to trade. These are often based on commodities or indexes2 such as crude oil, gold, or S&P 500 movements.

3. Day trading stocks requires at least $25,000, making this a more capital-intensive option.

What Can Be Traded?

The Most Lucrative And Popular Day Trading Markets Today Are:

1. Forex: The foreign exchange currency market is the world's most popular and liquid. The sheer volume of forex trading makes it attractive for day traders. There are multiple short-term opportunities in a trending currency pair, and an unrivaled level of liquidity to ensure opening and closing trades is quick and slick. More suited to technical analysis, there are other ways to trade foreign exchange. Also, forex has no central market. This means traders can make trades six days a week, 24 hours a day. They present a great starting point for entry-level or aspiring traders with full-time jobs. Traders in Australia might be specifically interested in trading the AUD USD pair.

2. Stocks: Physical stocks in individual companies, regular and Leveraged ETFs (an "Exchange Traded Fund" holds multiple stocks or commodities and is traded like a single stock), futures, and stock options. Trading stocks intraday offers different opportunities than a traditional 'buy and hold' strategy. Speculating on stock prices via CFDs or spread betting, for example, means traders can profit from falling prices too. Margin or leverage also reduce the capital required to open a position. So you can take a position on the latest news release, product announcement, or financial report – as well as technical indicators.

3. Cryptocurrencies: The two most popular currently are Bitcoin and Ethereum. The financial vehicle of the moment. Spectacular growth has seen cryptos attract many new investors.

Brokers are also ensuring retail access to these markets is less complicated. Taking a view on any of these new blockchain-based currencies is being simplified all the time. Barriers to entry are now almost nil, so whether you are a bull or a bear, now is the time.

4. Binary Options: The simplest and most predictable method, as the timing and return on a successful trade are known in advance. Regulatory changes are pending, and with the sector maturing, these products are now offered by big established brands. The only question for you is – will the asset rise in value, or not? With the downside limited to the size of the trade, and the potential payout known in advanced, understanding binaries is not difficult. They offer a different method of trading and can play a part in any day trader's daily portfolio.

5. Futures: The futures price of a commodity or security.

6. Commodities: Oil and natural gas, foodstuffs, metals, and minerals. If you're S&P 500 day trading, you'll be buying and selling the shares of companies, such as Starbucks and Adobe. In the day trading forex market, you'll be trading currencies, such as the Euro, U.S dollar, and GBP. In the futures market, often based on commodities and indexes, you can trade anything from gold to cocoa.

Index funds frequently occur in financial advice these days but are slow financial vehicles that make them unsuitable for daily trades. They have, however, been shown to be great for long-term investing plans. Another growing area of interest in the day trading world is a digital currency. Day trading with Bitcoin, LiteCoin, Ethereum, and other altcoins currencies is an expanding business. With lots of volatility, potential eye-popping returns, and an unpredictable future, day trading in cryptocurrency could be an exciting avenue to pursue.

Trading Accounts

Part of your day trading setup will involve choosing a trading account. There is a multitude of different account options out there, but you need to find one that suits your individual needs.

1. Cash Account: Day trading with a cash account (also known as without margin), will allow you to only trade the capital you have in your account. This limits your potential profits, but it also prevents you from losing more than you can afford.

2. Margin Account: This type of account allows you to borrow money from your broker. This will enable you to bolster your potential profits, but also comes with the risk of greater losses and rules to follow. If you want to start day trading with no minimum this isn't the option for you. Most brokerage firms will insist you lay down a minimum investment before you can start trading on margin. You can also experience a margin call, where your broker demands a greater deposit to cover potential losses. The broker's list has more detailed information on account options, such as day trading cash and margin accounts.

A Controversial Practice

The profit potential of day trading is perhaps one of the most debated and misunderstood topics on Wall Street. Internet day trading scams have lured amateurs by promising enormous returns in a short period. The idea that this kind of trading is a get-rich-quick scheme persists. Some people day trade without sufficient knowledge. But there are day traders who make a successful living despite or perhaps because of the risks.

Many professional money managers and financial advisors shy away from day trading arguing that, in most cases, the reward does not justify the risk. Conversely, those who do day trade insist there is profit to be made. Day trading profitably is possible, but the success rate is inherently lower because of the complexity and necessary risk of day trading in conjunction with the related scams. Moreover, economists and financial practitioners alike argue that over long periods, active trading strategies tend to underperform a more basic passive index strategy, especially after fees and taxes are taken into account.

Day trading is not for everyone and involves significant risks. Moreover, it requires an in-depth understanding of how the markets work and various strategies for profiting in the short term. While we remember the success stories of those who struck it rich as a day trader, remember that most do not many will fizzle out and many will just barely stay afloat. Furthermore, don't underestimate the role that luck and good timing play while skill is certainly an element, a rout of bad luck can sink even the most experienced day trader.

Day Trading vs The Alternatives

Yes, you have day trading, but with options like swing trading, traditional investing, and automation, how do you know which one to use?

1. Swing Trading: Swing traders usually make their play over several days or even weeks, which makes it different from day trading. It can still be a good method for the trader who wants to diversify.

2. Traditional Investing: Traditional investing is a longer game and looks to put money in popular assets such as stocks, bonds, and real estate for long-term value appreciation. Realistic investment returns over a whole year are in the 5-7% range. Unless you are already rich and can invest millions, traditional investing returns too little to make much of a difference daily. However, the intelligent trader will also invest long-term.

3. Robo-Advisors: An increasing number of people are turning to Robo-advisors. You simply chose an investing profile, then punch in your degree of risk and time frame for investing. Then an algorithm will do all the heavy lifting. This is normally a long-term investing plan and too slow for daily use.

Day trading vs long-term investing is two very different games. They require different strategies and mindsets. Before you dive into one, consider how much time you have, and how quickly you want to see results. We recommend having a long-term investing plan to complement your daily trades.

Terminology

Learn the trading lingo and vocabulary and you'll unlock the door to a whole host of trading secrets. Below we have collated the essential basic jargon, to create an easy to understand day trading glossary.

General

Leverage Rate: This is the rate your broker will multiply your deposit by, giving you buying power.

Automated Trading: Automated trading systems are programs that will automatically enter and exit trades based on a pre-programmed set of rules and criteria. They are also known as algorithmic trading systems, trading robots, or just bots.

Initial Public Offering (IPO): This is when a company sells a fixed number of shares to the market to raise capital.

Float: This is how many shares are available to trade. If a company releases 10,000 shares in the initial IPO, the float would be 10,000.

Beta: This numeric value measures the fluctuation of a stock against changes in the market.

Penny Stocks: These are any stocks trading below $5 a share.

Profit/Loss Ratio: Based on a percentage basis, this is the measure of a system's ability to generate profit instead of a loss.

Entry Points: This is the price at which you buy and enter your position.

Exit Points: This is the price at which you sell and exit your position.

Bull/Bullish: If you take a bullish position day trading you expect the stock to go up.

Bear/Bearish: If you take a bearish position you expect the stock to go down.

Market Trends: This is the general direction security is heading over a given time frame.

Hotkeys: These pre-programmed keys allow you to enter and exit trades rapidly, making them ideal if you need to exit a losing position as soon as possible.

Charts, Graphs, Patterns & Strategy

Support Level: This is the price level where the demand is strong enough that it prevents the decline in price past it.

Resistance Level: This is the price level where the demand is strong enough that selling the security will eradicate the increase in price.

Moving Averages: They provide you with vital buy and sell signals. Whilst they won't tell you in advance if a change is imminent, they will confirm if an existing trend is still in motion. Use them correctly and you can tap into a potentially profitable trend.

Relative Strength Index (RSI): Used to compare gains and losses over a specific period, it will measure the speed and change of the price movements of a security. In other words, it gives an evaluation of the strength of a security's recent price performance. Day trading tip – this index will help you identify oversold and overbought conditions in the trading of an asset, enabling you to steer clear of potential pitfalls.

Moving Average Convergence Divergence (MACD): This technical indicator calculates the difference between an instrument's two exponential moving averages. Using MACD can offer you straightforward buy and sell trading signals, making it popular amongst beginners.

Bollinger Bands: They measure the 'high' and 'low' of a price concerning previous trades. They can help with pattern recognition and enable you to arrive at systematic trading decisions.

Vix: This ticker symbol for the Chicago Board Options Exchange (CBOE), shows the expected volatility over the next 30 days.

Stochastics: Stochastic is the point of the current price concerning a price range over time. The method aims to predict when prices are going to turn by comparing the closing price of a security to its price range.

If you stumble across a word or phrase that leaves you scratching your head, refer back to this day trading dictionary and chances are you'll get a quick and easy explanation.

CHAPTER 2 - TIPS, DO'S AND DONT'S OF DAY TRADING

Day-Trading Rules

There are rules for every game, even day trading. If you are a new player, you must be mindful of the basic set of rules. These rules are certainly not binding, but they can help you to make some crucial decisions and give broader guidelines.

Knowledge

"Knowledge is power." Knowledge here includes information about the basic trading procedures and tools, information about stocks you plan to trade (like company financials, reports, and charts), knowing the latest in the stock markets, keeping track of events that affect stocks, etc. Day trading can become more difficult and risky in the absence of knowledge. Make a list of stocks that are on your wishlist, keep yourself informed about the selected companies and general markets, scan a business newspaper, and visit reliable financial websites regularly. An informed decision is a better decision.

Being Realistic

Being realistic about profits is important. As you gear up to trade, make sure that you don't lose out on decent gains in the greed for more. Markets are tricky, and it's better to settle down for a smaller profit than ending up losing heavily. Don't regret losing out on a chance. If required, you can always buy the same stock when it dips. Every small profitable trade will help boost your confidence and also give you a chance to try out the strategy again.

Margin Trading

Trading on margin means that you are borrowing money from a brokerage firm to trade. When appropriately used, margins help to amplify the trading results but amplification is not of profits, but of losses, as well if a trade goes against you. Keeping control of the amount of indulgence is vital, and trading with cash-in-hand helps to achieve that. To begin with, indulge in day trading without using margin. The high margin requirements for day trading on margin also act as a barrier for many to trading on margin.

Entry And Exit

Knowing the price at which you wish to enter and exit can help you book profits as well as save you from a wrong trade caused by unnecessary confusion. Don't play it by ear you must have some pre-fixed levels in your mind for every stock you plan to trade. In case the markets are not favorable, exit to cut losses.

Number of Stocks

As a beginner, it is advisable to focus on a maximum of one to two stocks during a day trading session. With just a few stocks, tracking and finding opportunities is easier. If you simultaneously trade with many stocks, you may miss out on chances to exit at the right time.

Rush Hours

Many orders placed by investors and traders begin to execute as soon as the markets open in the morning, and thus contribute to price volatility. A seasoned player may be able to recognize patterns and pick appropriately to make profits.

But as a novice, it is better to just read the market without making any moves for the first 15–20 minutes. The middle hours are usually less volatile while the movement again begins to pick toward the closing bell. Though the rush hours offer opportunities, as a novice, it's better to avoid that time to trade.

Set An Amount Aside

Day trading is risky, and there is a high chance of losses. Set aside a surplus amount of funds that you can trade with and are prepared to lose (which may not happen) while keeping the money for your basic living, expenses, etc. This will ensure that you are not increasing the risk quotient by neglecting your day-to-day needs while day trading.

Time

Above all else, day trading requires your time. Don't consider it as an option if you have limited hours to spare. The process requires a trader to track the markets and spot opportunities, which can arise at any time during the trading hours.

Avoid Penny Stocks

Keep away from penny stocks as a beginner in day trading. These stocks are highly illiquid, and chances of hitting the jackpot are often bleak. Don't trap yourself in a trade that is difficult to exit.

Limit Orders

When you place a market order, it is executed at the best price available at the time of execution. Thus there is no "price guarantee" in a market order. A limit order, meanwhile, does guarantee the price, but not the execution. Limit orders help you trade with more precision wherein you set your price (not unrealistic but executable) for buying as well as selling.

Unreliable Sources

Don't trust any SMS, mail, advertisement, etc. which makes claims about above-normal profits. It's not that all such sources are bogus, but authentication is required. As a rookie, be sure not to be tricked by someone lands you with a bad trade for a commission.

Emotion

There are times when the stock markets test your nerves. As a day trader, you need to learn to keep confidence, greed, hope, and fear at bay. The decisions should be governed by logic and not emotion. This may be hard for a beginner, but only someone who can learn to control his or her emotions can be successful. Before plunging into the real-time arena, it can be a good idea to try a simulation exercise. (Investopedia has a stock simulator here.)

Tips Of Day Trading

Day trading tips can come in a variety of forms. Each trader might want something different – from free stock tips to tips on tax when day trading. On this page, we have tried to collate as many useful tips as possible, including our "top 10". These range from psychology to strategy, money management to videos. So from beginners to advanced traders, we explain a range of free tips that can help intraday traders.

Top 10 Day Trading Tips

With a multitude of tips and tricks out there, what are the top 10 you should know about?

1. Always have a plan: The most important of all tips on day trading. Don't put real money on the line until you have a plan of action. That means know what you're buying and selling, how much you're going to trade and when you're going to trade it. A trader without a plan is a pig heading for an expensive slaughter.

2. Manage Risk: You must sit down and develop a risk management strategy. This will ensure you only lose what you can afford. Without one of these, your time as a day trader could be extremely short-lived.

3. Harness Technology: With thousands of other traders out there, you need to utilize all the resources around you to stay ahead. With that being said, charting platforms offer a huge number of ways to analyze the markets. You can also backtest your strategy against historical data to fill in any cracks. Mobile apps will also ensure you have instant access to the market, almost anywhere. Combine that with a lightning-fast internet connection and you can make fast, informed, and accurate decisions.

4. Never Stop Learning: The successful trader never sits on his laurels, he's always looking to trade smarter. Doing that means staying up to date with the news, utilizing trading books, and staying tuned into emerging schools of thought. Markets evolve and you need to evolve right along with them.

5. Lead With Facts: Make sure your strategy is based on, supported, and backtested with facts. Humans are emotional beings and after a big win today you may be feeling abnormally brave when the markets open tomorrow morning. Don't fall into this trap. Let facts and figures guide your decision-making processes.

6. Have Entry And Exit Rules: There is no such thing as the 'perfect entry and exit'. Stick only to the entry and exit parameters in your plan. If you start thinking 'maybe I should see if this works', think again. Maintain discipline and your bottom line will thank you for it.

7. Don't Concentrate On The Money: This may sound counterintuitive, but it makes good sense. Having money at the forefront of your mind could make you do reckless things, like taking tiny profits in fear of losing what you've already won, or jumping straight in so you don't miss a move. Instead, focus on sticking to your strategy and let your strategy focus on making you money.

---

8. Take Responsibility: Too many traders lose and then proclaim the market was out for them. By not taking responsibility you won't learn from your mistakes. Whatever happens, point the finger at yourself, in a constructive way. What did you do wrong? How can you stop it happening again? Do you need to amend your trading plan?

9. Keep A Trade Journal: Keeping a record of previous trades is an invaluable tip. Software now enables you to quickly and easily store all your trade history, from entry and exit to price and volume. You can use the information to identify problems and amend your strategy, enabling you to make intelligent decisions in the future. You never meet a trader who regrets keeping a trading journal.

10. Know When To Stop: If the strategy isn't working, don't keep throwing money at it. Go back to the drawing board and think again. If you can't stick to your plan, don't sit in the hot seat, you'll only start on a slippery and a dangerous slope, and there's no money at the end of it.

Tips For Beginners

As an aspiring trader, you may know some of the basics and have a decent idea of what you want to trade. But when the trading world is so full of variables, all of which can hinder your potential profits, you must learn and learn fast. Fortunately, I have collated the essential tips for beginners.

Picking A Market

Financial Considerations

One of the first decisions you'll have to make is deciding what you want to trade. Every market is different, bringing with them their benefits and drawbacks. You need at least $25,000 to start investing in the stock market for example, whereas the forex market requires the least amount of capital. You could start day trading with just $500 in your account.

So one of the first questions to answer is; how much capital do you have? Every market offers the potential for large profits, so don't think you have to trade stocks if you want to turn a profit. Also, bear in mind you'll likely lose some money to start with, so think about how much you're willing to spend.

Patience

One of the best tips on day trading for beginners is to stick to one market to start with. You don't need to invest in stocks, forex, and cryptocurrency all at once. Instead learn in-depth about one market, practice, learn from your mistakes, get good, and then consider adding another string to your trading bow. There's no rush, the markets aren't going anywhere. Devoting your time and energy into one market will help you maximize profits and minimize losses whilst you find your feet.

Essentials

Before you can start buying and selling Amazon and Google shares you need to ensure you have the basics. Those basics include:

1. A Reliable Internet Connection: Every second count when you're looking to capitalize on a high number of low value, intraday trades. You don't need your trade executions being hampered by an internet connection that cuts out. So use a cable and opt for at least a mid-range internet package.

2. A computer: One of the top tips for beginners is to have access to two monitors. If your computer crashes at a vital moment you could lose all your hard-earned profit. So have at least one relatively quick and reliable computer, preferably two.

3. A Trading Platform: You'll spend most of your day on here, so you need to ensure you choose a platform that suits your style and needs. Download a few different platforms and test them before you make up your mind. See our related page for more information on trading software.

4. A Broker: Your broker will be your gatekeeper to the market. They will facilitate your trades in return for a commission on your trades. When you're making so many trades each day, an expensive broker could seriously cut into your profits in the long term. Do your homework and find a broker that's reliable and offers a straightforward, competitive fee structure. To compare platforms, visit our broker's page.

Timing

Whilst some day traders are tuned in every day from 09:30 to 16:30 EST (for the U.S stock market), many trades for just a 2-3 hour window instead. As a beginner especially this will prevent you from making careless mistakes as your brain drops down a couple of gears when your concentration wanes. The hours you'll want to focus your attention on are as follows:

1. Forex Market: Although it trades 24-hours a day throughout the week, the most popular pair EUR/USD is most volatile between 06:00 and 17:00 GMT. In particular, 12:00 to 15:00 GMT sees the biggest price fluctuations.

2. Stock Market: You want to start early, within the first couple of hours of the market opening, and the last hour before it closes. So focus your attention between 09:30 and 13:30 EST and 15:00 to 16:00 EST. Again you'll see the most substantial price moves are made between these hours.

3. Futures Market: This is another market you want to hit early. 08:30 to 11:00 EST is when you'll find the best opportunities. Futures markets close at different times, so do your homework first. Bear in mind the last hour of trading also brings with it potential for profit.

Demo Accounts

An essential beginner's tip is to practice with a demo account first. They are usually funded with simulated money and they'll offer you a safe space to make mistakes and develop your strategies. They are also a fantastic place to get familiar with platforms, market conditions, and technical analysis. They're free and easy to use. What have you got to lose?

Final Word On Tips For Beginners

Utilizing these beginners' day trading tips will give you the best chance of succeeding when you take your first trading steps. You'll make mistakes, that's part of the game, but bear the above tips in mind and you may skip a lot of the initial hurdles.

Tips On Trading Psychology

You can have the best strategy in the world, but if you can't stay disciplined and keep your emotions in check, you risk losing profit. The first thing to note is that it's human nature to show and react with emotion, especially when there's money on the line. Fear, greed, and ambition are three of the most prevalent and potentially dangerous emotions. Fortunately, we have listed the top psychology tips to help you keep a level head.

1. Accept Losses: When you're making so many trades every day, you're bound to lose sometimes. It's how you respond to those losses that define your trading career. The loss trigger can quickly result in revenge trading, micro-managing, and just flat out poor decisions. Instead, embrace small losses and remember you're doing the correct thing, which is sticking to risk management.

2. Control Greed: Greed often influences traders in the following way; you enter a trade at $80 with a target of $95, but then it hits $95 and you think 'I'll just hold on a bit longer and increase profits further'. This only ends with you eventually losing big. The solution; stick rigidly to your strategy. Think long term and don't deviate from your strategy, there's simply no need to gamble.

3. Combat Fear: Yesterday was a bad day, you lost over $1,500 and the fear is now kicking in, you're being hesitant. That hesitation will cost you money, and as we mentioned above, you should embrace losses. When your confidence has had a knock, a useful tip is to remind yourself to stick religiously to your risk rules. If you have an effective risk management strategy you'll never lose more than you can afford.

4. Think Ahead: When you open a day trading psychology tips pdf, this will be one of the first things you'll see, and for good reason. Your strategy is to make money in the long run, so don't get focused on immediate results. Your strategy should cater to wins and losses, always keep the long-term process at the forefront of your mind.

Asset Specific Tips

Gold

Gold offers attractive price action when compared to say S&P 500. It's a popular choice amongst traders looking for consistent profits. Are there any day trading tips for gold though?

1. Correlation: This enables you to double-check your trade predictions. For example, gold is highly correlated to yen, as both are thought of as 'safe-haven instruments'. So you may be able to use other assets to support your decisions.

2. Look Outside: In today's global economy no markets move independently of each other, and gold is no exception. Make sure you stay abreast of developments in other markets that may affect your own trading decisions.

3. Consider Investor Sentiment: By checking traffic of gold-related websites, you can get a gauge for the current interest in the market. You can also monitor survey results and news events. All may help you make informed decisions.

Bitcoin

As the popularity of cryptocurrencies continues to climb, are there any specific tips you can apply to trade the most popular cryptocurrency of all, Bitcoin?

1. Understand Blockchain: Whilst you don't need a thorough understanding of the technical makeup of cryptocurrencies, understanding how blockchain works will only prove useful. Once you understand how they secure transactions (blocks) publicly and securely, you'll be in a better position to gauge the market's response to big news events. Such as a huge company incorporating blockchain technology into their everyday business operations.

2. Be Wary Of Volatility: Whilst volatility brings with it potential for profit, it also blurs your trading vision. Bitcoin is well known for being volatile so manage your risk carefully since you can't predict what's around the corner.

3. Know Other Altcoins: The success of Bitcoin depends on the success of its competitors. Understanding if they're growing or decreasing in popularity may help you predict future Bitcoin price movements.

Oil

A competitive market, but one that has seen many a trader retire with an extremely healthy looking bank balance. Are there any specific crude oil day trading tips then?

1. Exchange Rate: Crude oil is priced in US dollars, so the exchange rate is something to bear in mind when you're making short-term trades. For example, a weak US dollar sees an increase in the price of crude oil.

2. Supply & Demand: Consistent profits depend on consistent supply and demand. That means staying aware of domestic and international supply markets can come in useful. Resources such as the Baker-Hughes Oil rig count and the weekly US crude oil inventories can help you to that end.

3. Think Outside The Box: The US, Middle-East, China, Japan, India, and Russia are all important players on the oil stage. Unrest in one market could potentially impact the rest, so stay tuned into the geopolitical environment won't do any harm.

FTSE

Big names like Shell, Lloyds, and Tesco appeal to a mass of traders every single day. Are there any specific FTSE tips then that may help separate you from the rest?

1. Preparation: Make sure you're ready to go when the market opens. That means you're sat at your desk doing your homework well in advance of 08:00. If you fail to prepare, prepare to fail. It may sound cheesy, but that doesn't mean it's not true.

2. Quality vs Quantity: This is one of the most important FTSE 100 day trading tips. Many people think you have to trade in huge numbers to turn a profit. Yet many successful traders have been quick to point out it's better to have two or three good trades each day than a whole load of mediocre ones.

3. Beware Of The 1st: Many institutions like pension funds will commit large sums at the beginning of the month. Make sure any preparation you do takes anomaly days into account.

A quick Google and you'll also find daily tips for trading, ETFs, CFDs, options, and commodities. You'll probably also come across trading tips, strategies, and techniques in PDFs. However, the advice mentioned throughout this page and in the asset-specific tips above will apply to nearly all instruments.

India Day Trading Tips

Even the best tips may not be too useful if you're interested in markets on the other side of the world. If you want to become the next Rakesh Juhnjhunwala, who made over $2 billion from stocks, you may benefit from free and tailor-made tips for the Indian trader and market. Below are the essential intraday trading tips for India.

1. Trading Times: The NSE has a lot of similarities to other stock markets, including specific times when trading volume spikes. Between 09:30-14:30 UTC you need to dial into the market. If you're looking for volume and volatility, you won't want to leave your computer between these times.

2. Check Broker Fees: There is a vast disparity between commission fees charged by Indian brokers, so you must do your homework. Share Khan, TradeJini, Zerodha, and Sharekhan are all popular choices.

3. Utilize The News: Indian markets are extremely susceptible to news announcements, especially from big businesses and governments. Every second count when you're day trading, so you need a news outlet you can rely on. NDTV, Profit, Zee Awaaz, and ET are all highly regarded.

Whilst all these three tips are specifically for day trading in the Indian stock market, other tips on this page, like those on psychology, may also prove useful.

Taxes

Taxes like broker fees will cut into your profits, as will any penalties for failing to pay the correct dues. But, with so many differences between tax systems, knowing where you stand and what your obligations are isn't always straightforward. The best free tips, therefore, will help you maximize your profits whilst remaining within the parameters of tax laws.

Live Tips

Whilst you can look to videos for everything, from pattern to cash future option day trading tips, nothing beats getting hot off the press advice. If you can find a free trading share tips feed, you're onto a winner. There you can benefit from the experience of other traders in real-time as they react to the markets. Many brokerages and platforms, such as Tradingview.com, offer a safe space for traders to come together and brainstorm ideas.

Evaluating Tips

You'll find trading tips, hints, advice, and instructions all over the internet. But how do you know which ones to listen to and which ones to ignore? When you do read online tips and advice, there are three things to take into account:

1. Source: Where is the tip coming from? Is it from a reliable and impartial source? Or could the source have an ulterior motive, a brokerage advising you to go for a particular type of broker for example?

2. Timeframe: The efficacy of trading tips will vary depending on what type of trader they're aimed at. A strategy tip for long-term trading could have disastrous consequences if you apply it to intraday trading. Make sure you check the tips and advice are specific to the intraday trader.

3. Market-Specific: If you're day trading in the cryptocurrency market, consider whether the tip you've just read will be applicable when you're trading Bitcoin and Ethereum. Trading tips for the futures market may not only be useless when applied to the cryptocurrency market, they could hamper your strategy and increase your losses.

The Do's And Don'ts About Patience In Trading

Whether you're a newbie or an experienced trader, you surely have a clear concept in your mind about how being patient is a key factor in trading success. In my early days as a trader, I've been hearing about this concept so many times that I got lost on getting its pure meaning and, most importantly, I've initially failed to get the best practical instructions out of it. The main subject of this article is about giving you some pragmatic suggestions on how to implement patience into trading that helped me switching gears in my daily activity.

Going further in this article I want to dispel the myth that patience is synonymous with waiting. They are not and at the end of this reading I'm sure you're going to agree with me, so let's get into the details. Following here, there is a list of three dos and three don'ts where patience is involved trading.

Do's

1. Waiting for "A" quality setups only: Regardless of what's your favorite strategy is, someday trading opportunities will present themselves daily. If you take only the best out of those, you will only trade the best and leave the rest. At the same time, you won't mess up with overtrading or revenge trading. It has been proven

by many successful traders that trading more than 4-5 times per day on average doesn't give any profitable edge and can be counterproductive instead.

2. Looking for opportunities coming to you rather than the opposite: Here is another critical subject, once you have a clear picture of what a promising setup looks like based upon a proven strategy, use it as the input for your trading instead of hunting around many different stocks where you'd like to see a breakout/breakdown. Let it come to you because there is no benefit in forcing any kind of trades.

3. Respecting the original plan once you're in a trade: Plan the trade and trade the plan. Assuming that your trading strategy has a proven P/L ratio higher than 1:1, it means keeping your winning trades larger than your losing trades by only respecting what you know is working.

Don'ts

1. Waiting to stop out a losing trade: Here is the first huge difference between being patient and being stubborn. The first one is a great virtue, the second one isn't. Accepting the fact that trade didn't go the way you were looking for it to it's an emotional process that needs the practice to be implemented. The faster you'll get there, the sooner you'll be trimming your losses out considerably and you'll turn your trading consistently profitable.

2. Hesitating to jump in when a great setup stands out: This is a situation where I find myself more times than I'd like. Knowing that no trades have 100% of probability to work out in your favor, you've got to consistently trust the best setup when they occur. Hesitating too much not only will result in not taking a potential winning trade but also is a pre-requirement to another bad practice any trader wants to avoid which is chasing a trade. If you've missed the best entry (you can rest assured that it will continue to happen from time to time), do not get caught by the fear of missing out. Instead, just wait for the next promising setup before jumping in.

3. Rushing to take profit when a trade goes as for the plan: Here is another condition I'm quite confident every trader has experienced. In a rush of needing a winning trade, taking a much smaller profit than what it could have been once it is nicely going the way you were planning it to. So, be patient and let it work, especially once you've been good enough to put yourself in the driver's seat.

Trading Do's

1. Follow A Trading Plan: We have added this as the first item on the list for good reason. You need to have a solid plan that details every aspect of your trading before you venture into the Forex market. Remember that without a plan, you are not trading, you are gambling. Don't be a gambler – have a plan!

2. Have A Checklist: A checklist is number two on the list (it is almost as important as a trading plan!). On your checklist, include the trading rules that must be satisfied before you enter into a trade. This could be things like "trade is in the same direction as the overall market trend" or "reward: risk ratio is at least 3:1.", Reading through a checklist before each new trade greatly reduces your chances of making silly beginner mistakes.

3. Follow A Strict Routine: The importance of daily trading routine is something we have talked about before and for good reason. Trading can become a lonely endeavor, and some may struggle with a completely new situation where they have no boss to tell them what to do at all times. Having a routine in place will help you overcome these challenges and put you on track for a successful career as an independent trader.

Trading Don'ts

1. Become Emotional: Becoming either angry when you lose or overly happy each time you make money is not a recipe for success as a forex trader. It is a fact that the best traders among us are those who can detach their emotions completely from their trading. It is when you become emotional that you make the worst mistakes in trading, such as trying to make up for a loss, becoming overly aggressive after a win, and so on. In short, this only leads to bad outcomes for forex traders. Don't get carried away!

2. Marry A Trade: Sometimes in trading, you become so convinced that a certain trading instrument will move either up or down that you completely ignore arguments and even evidence of the contrary.

For example, don't buy Apple shares purely out of your love for iPhones. You may love your phone, but as traders, we need to look at trading opportunities objectively to succeed.

3. Listen To Rumors: In trading, you must remember to always do your research. Perhaps you have a friend who's good at trading and has made lots of money, but your situation will still always be slightly different: You don't follow the same trading strategy and methodology, you don't have the same position size, and you may not know the target price or stop-loss that he is using.

CHAPTER 3 - DAY TRADING AND SWING TRADING

Day Trading Vs. Swing Trading: What's The Difference?

Day Trading

Day trading, as the name suggests, involves making dozens of trades in a single day, based on technical analysis and sophisticated charting systems. The day trader's objective is to make a living from trading stocks, commodities, or currencies, by making small profits on numerous trades and capping losses on unprofitable trades. Day traders typically do not keep any positions or own any securities overnight.

The biggest lure of day trading is the potential for spectacular profits. But this may only be possible for the rare individual who possesses all the necessary traits, such as decisiveness, discipline, and diligence, required to become a successful day trader. The day trader works alone, independent from the whims of corporate bigwigs. He can have a flexible working schedule, take time off whenever needed, and work at his own pace, unlike someone on the corporate treadmill.

Day traders have to compete with high-frequency traders, hedge funds, and other market professionals who spend millions to gain trading advantages. In this environment, a day trader has little choice but to spend heavily on a trading platform, charting software, state-of-the-art computers, and the like. Ongoing expenses include costs for obtaining live price quotes and commission expenses that can add up because of the volume of trades.

Long-time day traders love the thrill of pitting their wits against the market and other professionals day in and day out. The adrenaline rush from rapid-fire trading is something not many traders will admit to, but it is a big factor in their decision to make a living from day trading. It's doubtful these kinds of people would be content spending their days selling widgets or poring over numbers in an office cubicle. To make a go at it, a day trader must quit his day job and give up his steady monthly paycheck. From then on, the day trader must depend entirely on his skill and efforts to generate enough profit to pay the bills and enjoy a decent lifestyle.

Day trading is stressful because of the need to watch multiple screens to spot trading opportunities, and then act quickly to exploit them. This has to be done day after day, and the requirement for such a high degree of focus and concentration can often lead to burnout. For many jobs in finance, having the right degree from the right university is a prerequisite just for an interview. Day trading, in contrast, does not require an expensive education from an Ivy League school. While there are no formal educational requirements for becoming a day trader, courses in technical analysis and computerized trading may be very helpful.

Key Takeaways

❖ Day trading, as the name suggests, involves making dozens of trades in a single day, based on technical analysis and sophisticated charting systems.

❖ Swing trading is based on identifying swings in stocks, commodities, and currencies that take place over days.

❖ Neither strategy is better than the other, and traders should choose the approach that works best for their skills, preferences, and lifestyle.

Swing Trading

Swing trading is based on identifying swings in stocks, commodities, and currencies that take place over days. A swing trade may take a few days to a few weeks to work out. Unlike a day trader, a swing trader is not likely to make trading a full-time career, though a trader might choose to be a day trader AND a swing trader.

Anyone with knowledge and investment capital can try swing trading. Because of the longer time-frame (from days to weeks as opposed to minutes to hours), a swing trader does not need to be glued to his computer screen all day. He can even maintain a separate full-time job (as long as he is not checking trading screens all the time at work).

Trades generally need time to work out. Keeping a trade for an asset open for a few days or weeks may result in higher profits than trading in and out of the same security multiple times a day.

Since swing trading usually involves positions held at least overnight, margin requirements are higher. Maximum leverage is usually two times one's capital. Compare this with day trading where margins are four times one's capital. The swing trader can set stop losses. While there is a risk of a stop being executed at an unfavorable price, it beats the constant monitoring of all open positions that are a feature of day trading.

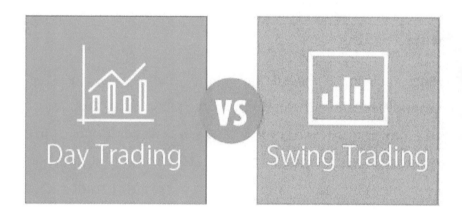

As with any style of trading, swing trading can also result in substantial losses. Because swing traders hold their positions for longer than day traders, they also run the risk of larger losses. Since swing trading is seldom a full-time job, there is much less chance of burnout due to stress. Swing traders usually have a regular job or another source of income from which they can offset or mitigate trading losses. Swing trading can be done with just one computer and conventional trading tools. It does not require the state-of-the-art technology of day trading.

Key Differences

Day trading and swing trading each have advantages and drawbacks. Neither strategy is better than the other, and traders should choose the approach that works best for their skills, preferences, and lifestyle. Day trading is better suited for individuals who are passionate about trading full time and possess the three Ds: decisiveness, discipline, and diligence (prerequisites for successful day trading).

Day trading success also requires an advanced understanding of technical trading and charting. Since day trading is intense and stressful, traders should be able to stay calm and control their emotions under fire. Finally, day trading involves risk traders should be prepared to sometimes walk away with 100 percent losses.

Swing trading, on the other hand, does not require such a formidable set of traits. Since swing trading can be undertaken by anyone with some investment capital and does not require full-time attention, it is a viable option for traders who want to keep their full-time jobs, but also dabble in the markets. Swing traders should also be able to apply a combination of fundamental and technical analysis, rather than technical analysis alone.

Day Trading Versus Swing Trading – Which Is Better?

Day Trading Or Swing Trading That Is The Question.

If you are an active trader, day trading and swing trading will feel like second cousins. At the end of the day, both trading methodologies seek to make short-term profits based on price fluctuations in the market. In this article, I will provide key differentials that will assist you in determining if one is better suited for your risk profile

1 Level of Effort Required

Day Trading

Day trading requires that you practically give you're firstborn during trading hours. You'll be hard press to even take a bathroom break. You are required to analyze the market every day and make quick decisions. You will likely trade during specific time frames (e.g. morning or afternoon). There are the brave few who can trade all day and still turn a profit but let me tell you from experience the headaches from staring at the screen all day is excruciating. Without a doubt when you are day trading you should not be multitasking with the television or talking on the phone.

Swing Trading

Swing trading at least allows you to take a breath. While you still have to watch your stocks to ensure key levels are not breached, you do not have to hawk the tape like a mad person. Without offending the swing traders of the world, I would dare to say you can swing trade on a part-time basis and still turn a profit. You may have fewer trade decisions to make, but you are expected to develop a thorough trading plan with entry and exit points.

2. Number Of Trades Per Day

Day Trading

Day trading means you open and close trades during the same day. You could trade as few as once per day up to a hundred or more trades. I believe that if you are manually trading, the more you trade, the greater chance you have of losing money over time. Therefore I only like to place 3 to 5 trades per day.

Swing Trading

Swing Trading does not require you to place trades daily. Generally, trades are placed every 2 to 3 weeks. The lengthier time is because you need to provide the stock the ability to "swing" from one price point to the next. Now, there are times when stock will just have a breakaway gap and you will, of course, hold off on the 2 to the 3-week timeline and just let the stock run.

3. Money Management

Day Trading

Day trading allows you to use up to 4 times your available cash to buy and sell securities. This means as a small-time trader with a 100k in the capital you can now trade up to 400k during the day. I do not use all of the money available because of how great it increases my risk profile. You are required to make quick decisions on how much money you will allocate per trade. This requires you to track how much of your money is in float and also have an understanding of the margin requirements of your brokerage firm.

Swing Trading

Swing trading allows you to trade with a maximum of two times your available cash. No matter what time frame or style of trading you prefer, the money management principles are the same:

- ❖ Never have too much money in one position
- ❖ Use margin sparingly
- ❖ Always have a stop loss open or at least in your mind of when you pull the trigger
- ❖ Make Money out of the market. If you never pull out money, it will never find its way to your wallet.

4. Risks

Day Trading

Since everyone that reads Tradingsim knows I prefer day trading, I'm guessing you know what I'm going to say here. Day trading on the surface sounds riskier, but in actuality, day trading provides you far more control over your trading activity. When I am in a position, I am literally in a position.

I have my monitors going, time, and sales streaming and are watching the stock go through its gyrations. This level of monitoring means I gain a feel for how hard the stock is trending and can quickly pull the trigger if things go to the left. Where day trading gets riskier is when it comes to your money management principles covered under 4 above. Because you have more leverage there is a greater chance you can get yourself in trouble.

My golden ratio was to never use more than 10% of my available margin on any trade. As your account value increases in size and therefore your per trade profits, you should naturally reduce the amount of margin you use to improve your risk profile. That is unless greed gets a hold of you and you start to believe there is always more.

Swing Trading

Swing trading has the exact opposite risk profile. Since you have less margin to use per trade, this naturally reduces your risk;

however, swing trades expose you to holding positions overnight. For me, this introduces too much risk relative to day trading. Most news events such as earnings, public relations announcements, or analyst recommendations occur outside of normal trading hours. I cannot risk waking up and seeing my stock has gapped down 20% from the previous days' close.

5. Instant Gratification

Day Trading

I like to do work around the house and in the yard when it comes to small jobs. When I say small, I'm talking about cutting the grass or changing the light bulb. The reason being, I get an immediate sense of accomplishment. I set out to perform a task and I can quickly see the results of my efforts. This is another reason I am a fan of day trading. I can measure my performance daily. There is no ambiguity around how much I can make this month or quarter. I know every day whether I was a winner or not.

Swing Trading

Swing trading requires you to have more patience, which I do not like to wait for things. You may hold your trade for a few days or 8 weeks. It depends on how well the stock trends. The periods where it is unknown whether I will close the trade out with a profit increases my anxiety levels to a point outside of my comfort zone. Are you willing to hold positions for weeks or a few months?

6. Startup Capital Required

Day Trading

I say this every article to make sure my readers understand this point clearly. You need starting capital of 50 to 1, cash to expenses to begin a career as a day trader. The only reason this rule bends at all is if you have supplemental income which you can use to offset your monthly expenses. Therefore, if you have 3k a month in bills, you need $150k cash to day trade. This sounds like a lot and it is. The end goal here is to ensure you can make it in day trading over the long haul and not go broke.

Swing Trading

Since you can swing trade and still hold down a full-time job, the amount of money required is really up to you and your financial responsibilities. If you are planning on swing trading for a living I would say you need 100 to 1 cash to expenses. The reason for the increase is you may be in a trade for longer than one month and are unable to use trading profits to pay your living expenses. With this ratio you are only losing 1 percent of your trading capital per month in the event you are in a position a little longer than expected.

Focus, Time, And Practice

Swing trading and day trading both require a good deal of work and knowledge to generate profits consistently, although the knowledge required isn't necessarily "book smarts." Successful trading results from finding a strategy that produces an edge, or a profit over a significant number of trades, and then executing that strategy over and over again.

Some knowledge on the market being traded and one profitable strategy can start generating income, along with lots and lots of practice. Each day prices move differently than they did on the last, which means the trader needs to be able to implement their strategy under various conditions and adapt as conditions change.

This presents a difficult challenge, and consistent results only come from practicing a strategy under loads of different market scenarios. That takes time and should involve making hundreds of trades in a demo account before risking real capital. Choosing day trading or swing trading also comes down to personality. Day trading typically involves more stress, requires sustained focus for extended periods, and takes incredible discipline. People that like action, have fast reflexes, and/or like video games and poker tend to gravitate toward day trading.

Swing trading happens at a slower pace, with much longer lapses between actions like entering or exiting trades. It can still be high stress, and also requires immense discipline and patience. It doesn't require as much sustained focus, so if you have difficulty staying focused, swing trading may be the better option. Fast reflexes don't matter in swing trading as trades can be taken after the market closes and prices have stopped moving.

Day trading and swing trading both offer freedom in the sense that a trader is their boss. Traders typically work on their own, and they are responsible for funding their accounts and for all losses and profits generated. One can argue that swing traders have more freedom in terms of time because swing trading takes up less time than day trading.

Should I Be A Day Trader Or A Swing Trader?

A large part of this decision is no real decision at all because it is determined by economics and time. Most people need to work full-time to meet their financial obligations and even good traders will report wide fluctuations between their gains and losses over time. This means that almost everyone can rule out full-time day trading as a realistic possibility. It might be that you have some time, perhaps a couple of hours, which you could dedicate exclusively and intensively to trading every day. However, you must ask yourself whether this is the "right" time – if it does not correspond with either the Tokyo, London, or New York openings, it won't be. Furthermore, you will meet more market opportunities being plugged in once every few hours continuously, then you will by being plugged in for a couple of hours each. This is just the way the market works. If you are determined to become a day trader, I think most day traders would agree with me when I say that if you can't master swing trading, you won't master day trading, so that should make it clear what style you should start with, at least.

A Final Comparison

One trading style isn't better than the other; they just suit differing needs. Day trading has more profit potential, at least in percentage terms on smaller-sized trading accounts. Swing traders have a better chance of maintaining their percentage returns even as their account grows, up to a certain point. Capital requirements vary quite a bit across the different markets and trading styles. Day trading requires more time than swing trading, while both take a great deal of practice to gain consistency. Day trading makes the best option for action lovers. Those seeking a lower-stress and less time-intensive option can embrace swing trading.

Day trading risk management generally follows the same template or line of thinking. It is most commonly some form of the "one percent rule". Namely, it is a rules-based system stipulating that no more than one percent of your account can be dedicated to any given trade. This is done as a matter of prudently managing capital and keeping losses to a minimum.

The "one percent rule" ensures that a trader's "off days", or scenarios where the market goes against the trades in the account, don't damage the portfolio more than necessary. Effective day trading risk management is the most important skill to learn. And much of what's involved in sustaining gains over the long run means avoiding material losses of capital. Keeping your losses shallow is imperative. When losses deepen, this is also usually when psychology starts playing more of a role, and always in an adverse way. Traders start making worse decisions and can spiral into a "risk of ruin" scenario.

Everything is a probability. Accordingly, you want to avoid betting too much on any given thing, because there is the chance that it'll go against you. The general strategy in trading or investing more broadly is to make multiple uncorrelated bets where the probability is in your favor. If you can execute this, you will be successful.

Risk Management

As a day trader, risk management is just as important as developing a solid trading strategy. No day trader is perfect and all day traders will inevitably have losing trades. A fine-tuned risk management strategy is what gives traders the ability to lose on trades without causing irreparable damage to their accounts. Think of it this way. A day trader can have a 50% win rate and still be profitable if they're average profit is twice the amount of their average loss. Contrarily, another trader may have a 75% win rate with average losses that are four times higher than their average profits. Have a look at the formula below to better understand the concept.

Long-Term Profitability Formula

This formula can be used to determine a trader's long-term profitability. Using this formula, let's compare the outcome of 2 different traders who each place 10 trades:

Trader A

- ❖ 50% Win Rate
- ❖ 50% Loss Rate
- ❖ $200 Average Profit
- ❖ $100 Average Loss
- ❖ [($200)(0.5)]*10 - [($100)(0.5)]*10= $500 Profit

Trader B

- ❖ 75% Win Rate
- ❖ 25% Loss Rate
- ❖ $100 Average Profit
- ❖ $400 Average Loss
- ❖ [($100)(0.75)]*10 - [($400)(0.25)]*10= -$250 Loss

Even though Trader B has a higher win rate, he is not profitable due to a poor risk management strategy. What is the point of this? Limiting losses is just as valuable as increasing your win rate and, generally speaking, it is much easier to limit losses than it is to increase your win rate.

What Is Risk?

Risk is defined in financial terms as the chance that an outcome or investment's actual gains will differ from an expected outcome or return. Risk includes the possibility of losing some or all of the original investment. Quantifiably, the risk is usually assessed by considering historical behaviors and outcomes. In finance, the standard deviation is a common metric associated with risk. Standard deviation provides a measure of the volatility of asset prices in comparison to their historical averages in a given time frame.

Overall, it is possible and prudent to manage to invest risks by understanding the basics of risk and how it is measured. Learning the risks that can apply to different scenarios and some of the ways to manage them holistically will help all types of investors and business managers to avoid unnecessary and costly losses.

What Are the Main Risks Associated With Trading Derivatives?

Derivatives are investment instruments that consist of a contract between parties whose value derives from and depends on the value of an underlying financial asset. However, like any investment instrument, there are varying levels of risk associated with derivatives. Among the most common derivatives traded are futures, options, contracts for difference, or CFDs, and swaps. This article will cover derivatives risk at a glance, going through the primary risks associated with derivatives: market risk, counterparty risk, liquidity risk, and interconnection risk.

Market Risk

Market risk refers to the general risk of any investment. Investors make decisions and take positions based on assumptions, technical analysis, or other factors that lead them to certain conclusions about how an investment is likely to perform. While there is not a surefire way to protect against market risk, as all are vulnerable to changes in the market, knowing how much a derivative is impacted by market fluctuations will help investors choose wisely. In reality, an important part of investment analysis is determining the probability of investment being profitable and assessing the risk/reward ratio of potential losses against potential gains.

Counterparty Risk

Counterparty risk, or counterparty credit risk, arises if one of the parties involved in a derivatives trade, such as the buyer, seller or dealer, defaults on the contract. This risk is higher in over-the-counter, or OTC, markets, which are much less regulated than ordinary trading exchanges. A regular trading exchange helps facilitate contract performance by requiring margin deposits that are adjusted daily through the mark-to-market process. The mark-to-market process makes pricing derivatives more likely to accurately reflect current value. Traders can manage counterparty risk by only using dealers they know and consider trustworthy.

Liquidity Risk

Liquidity risk applies to investors who plan to close out a derivative trade before maturity. Overall, liquidity risk refers to the ability of a company to pay off debts without big losses to its business. To measure liquidity risk, investors compare short-term liabilities and the company's liquid assets. Firms that have low liquidity risk can quickly turn their investments into cash to prevent a loss. Liquidity risk is also important for investors interested in derivatives to consider. Such investors need to consider if it is difficult to close out the trade or if existing bid-ask spreads are so large as to represent a significant cost.

Interconnection Risk

Interconnection risk refers to how the interconnections between various derivative instruments and dealers might affect an investor's particular derivative trade. Some analysts express concern over the possibility that problems with just one party in the derivatives market, such as a major bank that acts as a dealer, might lead to a chain reaction or snowball effect that threatens the stability of financial markets overall.

Risk Management Techniques For Active Traders

Risk management helps cut down losses. It can also help protect a trader's account from losing all of his or her money. The risk occurs when the trader suffers a loss. If it can be managed, the trader can open him or herself up to making money in the market. It is an essential but often overlooked prerequisite to successful active trading. After all, a trader who has generated substantial profits can lose it all in just one or two bad trades without a proper risk management strategy. So how do you develop the best techniques to curb the risks of the market?

This article will discuss some simple strategies that can be used to protect your trading profits.

Planning Your Trades

As Chinese military general Sun Tzu's famously said: "Every battle is won before it is fought." This phrase implies that planning and strategy not the battles win wars. Similarly, successful traders commonly quote the phrase: "Plan the trade and trade the plan." Just like in war, planning can often mean the difference between success and failure.

First, make sure your broker is right for frequent trading. Some brokers cater to customers who trade infrequently. They charge high commissions and don't offer the right analytical tools for active traders.

Stop-loss (S/L) and take-profit (T/P) points represent two key ways in which traders can plan when trading. Successful traders know what price they are willing to pay and at what price they are willing to sell. They can then measure the resulting returns against the probability of the stock hitting their goals. If the adjusted return is high enough, they execute the trade.

Conversely, unsuccessful traders often enter a trade without having any idea of the points at which they will sell at a profit or a loss. Like gamblers on a lucky or unlucky streak emotions begin to take over and dictate their trades. Losses often provoke people to hold on and hope to make their money back, while profits can entice traders to imprudently hold on for even more gains.

Consider the One-Percent Rule

A lot of day traders follow what's called the one-percent rule. This rule of thumb suggests that you should never put more than 1% of your capital or your trading account into a single trade. So if you have $10,000 in your trading account, your position in any given instrument shouldn't be more than $100. This strategy is common for traders who have accounts of less than $100,000 some even go as high as 2% if they can afford it. Many traders whose accounts have higher balances may choose to go with a lower percentage. That's because as the size of your account increases, so too does the position. The best way to keep your losses in check is to keep the rule below 2% any more and you'd be risking a substantial amount of your trading account.

Setting Stop-Loss And Take-Profit Points

A stop-loss point is a price at which a trader will sell a stock and take a loss on the trade. This often happens when a trade does not pan out the way a trader hoped. The points are designed to prevent the "it will come back" mentality and limit losses before they escalate. For example, if a stock breaks below a key support level, traders often sell as soon as possible. On the other hand, a take-profit point is a price at which a trader will sell a stock and make a profit on the trade. This is when the additional upside is limited given the risks. For example, if a stock is approaching a key resistance level after a large move upward, traders may want to sell before a period of consolidation takes place.

How To More Effectively Set Stop-Loss Points

Setting stop-loss and take-profit points are often done using technical analysis, but fundamental analysis can also play a key role in timing. For example, if a trader is holding a stock ahead of earnings as excitement builds, he or she may want to sell before the news hits the market if expectations have become too high, regardless of whether the take-profit price has been hit.

Moving averages represent the most popular way to set these points, as they are easy to calculate and widely tracked by the market. Key moving averages include the 5-, 9-, 20-, 50-, 100- and 200-day averages. These are best set by applying them to a stock's chart and determining whether the stock price has reacted to them in the past as either a support or resistance level.

Another great way to place stop-loss or take-profit levels is on support or resistance trend lines. These can be drawn by connecting previous highs or lows that occurred on significant, above-average volume. Like with moving averages, the key is determining levels at which the price reacts to the trend lines and, of course, on high volume.

When Setting These Points, Here Are Some Key Considerations:

❖ Use longer-term moving averages for more volatile stocks to reduce the chance that a meaningless price swing will trigger a stop-loss order to be executed.

❖ Adjust the moving averages to match target price ranges. For example, longer targets should use larger moving averages to reduce the number of signals generated.

❖ Stop losses should not be closer than 1.5-times the current high-to-low range (volatility), as it is too likely to get executed without reason.

- ❖ Adjust the stop loss according to the market's volatility. If the stock price isn't moving too much, then the stop-loss points can be tightened.

- ❖ Use known fundamental events such as earnings releases, as key periods to be in or out of a trade as volatility and uncertainty can arise.

Calculating Expected Return

Setting stop-loss and take-profit points are also necessary to calculate the expected return. The importance of this calculation cannot be overstated, as it forces traders to think through their trades and rationalize them. As well, it gives them a systematic way to compare various trades and select only the most profitable ones. This can be calculated using the following formula:

"[(Probability of Gain) x (Take Profit % Gain)] + [(Probability of Loss) x (Stop-Loss % Loss)]"

The result of this calculation is an expected return for the active trader, who will then measure it against other opportunities to determine which stocks to trade. The probability of gain or loss can be calculated by using historical breakouts and breakdowns from the support or resistance levels—or for experienced traders, by making an educated guess.

Diversify And Hedge

Making sure you make the most of your trading means never putting your eggs in one basket. If you put all your money in one stock or one instrument, you're setting yourself up for a big loss. So remember to diversify your investments—across both industry sector as well as market capitalization and geographic region. Not only does this help you manage your risk, but it also opens you up to more opportunities. You may also find yourself a time when you need to hedge your position. Consider a stock position when the results are due. You may consider taking the opposite position through options, which can help protect your position. When trading activity subsides, you can then unwind the hedge.

Downside Put Options

If you are approved for options trading, buying a downside put option, sometimes known as a protective put, can also be used as a hedge to stem losses from a trade that turns sour. A put option gives you the right, but not the obligation, to sell the underlying stock at a specified price at or before the option expires. Therefore if you own XYZ stock from $100 and buy the 6-month $80 put for $1.00 per option in premium, then you will be effectively stopped out from any price drop below $79 ($80 strike minus the $1 premium paid).

9 Tips That Will Improve Your Risk Management Right Now

Risk management usually ranks very low on the priorities list of most traders. Typically, way behind finding a better indicator, more accurate entry signals, or worrying about stop hunting and unfair Algo-trading practices. However, without proper knowledge about risk management, profitable trading is impossible. A trader needs to understand how to manage his risk, size his positions, create a positive outlook for his performance, and set his orders correctly if he wants to become a profitable and professional trader.

Here are 9 tips that will help you improve your risk management instantly and avoid the most common problems that cause traders to lose money.

1. Setting Orders And The Reward: Risk Ratio

When you spot an entry signal, think where you'd place your stop loss and take profit order FIRST. Once you've identified reasonable price levels for your orders, measure the risk: reward ratio. If it doesn't match your requirements, skip the trade. Don't try to widen your take profit order or tighten your stop loss to achieve a higher reward: risk ratio.

"The reward of a trade is always uncertain and potential. The risk is the only thing you can control about your trade."

Most amateur traders do this the opposite way: they come up with a random reward: risk ratio and then manipulate their stop and profit orders to achieve their ratio.

2. Avoid Break-Even Stops

Moving the stop loss to the point of the entry and so creating a "no risk" trade is a very dangerous and often unprofitable maneuver. Whereas it's good and advisable to protect your position, the break-even strategy often leads to a variety of problems.

Especially if you are trading based on common technical analysis (support/resistance, chart patterns, highs, and lows, or moving averages), your point of entry is usually very obvious and many traders will have a very similar entry. Of course, the pros know that and you can often see that price retraces back and squeezes the amateurs at the very obvious price levels, just before price then turns back into the original direction. A break-even stop will get out of potentially profitable trades if you move your stop too soon.

3. Never Even Use Fixed Stop Distances

Many trading strategies tell you to use a fixed amount of points/pips on your stop loss and take profit orders across different instruments and even markets. Those "shortcuts" and generalizations completely neglect how price moves naturally and how financial markets work.

Volatility and momentum are constantly changing and, therefore, how much price moves in any given day and how much it fluctuates changes all the time. In times of higher volatility, you should set your stop loss and take profit orders wider to avoid premature stop runs and to maximize profits when price swings more. And in times of low volatility, you have to set your orders closer to your entry and not be overly optimistic.

Secondly, trading with fixed distances doesn't let you chose reasonable price levels and it also takes away all the flexibility you need to have as a trader. Always be aware of important price levels and barriers such as round numbers, big moving averages, Fibonacci levels, or just plain support and resistance.

4. Always Compare Win Rate And Reward: Risk Together

Many traders claim that figure win rate is useless. But those traders miss a very important point. While observing the win rate alone will provide you with no valuable insights, combining win rate and risk: reward ratio can be seen as the holy grail in trading. It's so important to understand that you neither need an insanely high win rate or have to ride your trades for a very long time. For example, a system with a win rate of 40% (which is what many professional traders average) only requires a reward: risk ratio of greater than 1.6 to trade profitably. Trying to achieve an astronomical high win rate or believing that you have to ride trades for a long time often create wrong expectations and then leads to wrong assumptions and, finally, to mistakes in how traders approach their trading.

5. Don't Use Daily Performance Targets

Many traders will randomly set daily or weekly performance targets. Such an approach is very dangerous and you have to stop thinking in terms of daily or weekly returns. Setting yourself daily goals creates a lot of pressure and it usually also creates a "need to trade". Instead, here are some ideas on how to set trading goals the right way:

1. **Short-Term (Daily And Weekly):** Focus on the best possible trade execution and on how well you follow your rules/plan.

2. **Mid-Term (Weekly And Monthly):** Follow a professional routine, plan your trades, obey your rules, journal your trades, review your trades, and make sure that you learn the correct lessons.

3. Longer-Term (Semiannually): Review your trades, focusing on how well you executed your trades to get an understanding of your level of professionalism. Find weaknesses in your trading and adjust accordingly. This will lead to profitable trading inevitably.

6. Position Sizing Like A Pro

When it comes to position sizing, traders usually pick a random number such as 1%, 2%, or 3%, and then apply it to all their trades without ever thinking about position sizing again. Trading is an activity of chance, such as professional betting or poker. In those activities, it's common practice to vary the amount you wager, based on the likelihood of the outcome. If you hold a very strong hand in poker, you'd bet more than when you see almost no chances of winning, right?

The same holds for trading. If you trade multiple setups or strategies, you will see that each setup and strategy has a different win rate and also that the reward: risk ratios on different strategies vary. Thus, you should reduce your position size on setups with a lower win rate and increase the position size when your win rate is higher. Following the approach of dynamic position sizing will help you reduce your account volatility and potentially help you improve account growth.

7. Using The Reward: Risk Ratio And R-Multiple Together

Whereas the reward: risk ratio is more of a potential metric where you measure the distances to your stop and profit target when you enter the trade, the R-multiple is a performance measurement and it describes the outcome of your trades. When entering trades, traders are often too optimistic and set profit targets too far or close their profitable trades too early which will then decrease their initial reward: risk ratio. By analyzing how your R-multiple compares to your reward: risk ratio, you can get new insights into your trading. If you see major deviations, you should look deeper and try to find what is causing the differences.

8. Take Spread Seriously

For the most liquid instruments, spreads are usually just a few pips and, therefore, traders view them as they weren't even existent. Research shows that only about 1% of all day traders can profit net of fees.

The average day trader usually holds his trades for anywhere between 5 and 200 pips. If the spread on your instrument is 2 pips, this will mean that you pay a fee of 10% on trades with a profit of 20 pips. And even if you hold your trade for 50 pips, the spread amounts to almost 5%. Those costs can result in significant drawbacks for your trading system and even turn winning into a losing system. Therefore, start monitoring spread closely and avoid instruments or times where spreads are high.

9. Correlations – Increasing Risk Unknowingly

If you are a forex trader, you can often see a very strong correlation between certain forex pairs. If you are a stock trader, you will notice that companies within the same industries and sectors, or which are based in the same country, often move together over long periods. When it comes to money- and risk management this means that trading instruments that are positively correlated lead to increased risk. Let's illustrate this with an example:

Let's say you bought the EUR/USD and the GBP/USD, and you are risked 1.5% on each trade; the correlation between those 2 instruments is highly positive (close to +0.90). This means that if the EUR/USD goes up 1%, the GBP/USD goes up 0.90% as well. Having a long position in both the EUR/USD and the GBP/USD is then equal to having 1 position open and risking 2.7% on it [(1.5%+1.5%)*0.9=2.7%]. Of course, this is a very simplistic way of looking at correlations, but it gives you an idea of what to keep in mind when trading correlated instruments.

Day Trading Platforms

Day Trading, which is buying and selling shares during the same trading session, exploded in popularity back in the booming stock market of the 1990s. Everyone was trying to get in and out of securities and make a profit on an intraday basis. After the dot-com market crash in 2000, the SEC and FINRA established the "Pattern Day Trader" rule in 2001, which increased the requirements to day trade to better protect consumers.

Today trade today, you have at least $25,000 to comply with the Pattern Day Trader rule. Traders must also meet margin requirements. The government put these laws into place to protect investors. Bottom line: day trading is risky. Today trade effectively, you need to choose a day trading platform. As a day trader, you need a combination of low-cost trades coupled with a feature-rich trading platform and great trading tools. Price isn't everything; therefore, many day traders are willing to pay more to get the tools they need to trade more efficiently.

Best Trading Platforms

Here's a breakdown of some of the best online brokers for day trading.

- ❖ Trade Station: Best platform technology
- ❖ TD Ameritrade: Best desktop platform
- ❖ Interactive Brokers: Best for professionals
- ❖ Fidelity: Best order execution
- ❖ E-TRADE: A best web-based platform

Trade Station Best Platform Technology

As a trading technology leader, TradeStation shines, supporting traders through its web-based platform as well as its desktop platform, which we rated No. 1 for Platform Technology. Both are excellent. Tools in the TradeStation arsenal include Radar Screen (real-time streaming watch lists with 329 customizable columns), Scanner (custom screening), Matrix (ladder trading), and Walk-Forward Optimizer (advanced strategy testing), among others. Using TradeStation's proprietary coding language, EasyLanguage, traders can even code their apps for the platform and make them available in TradeStation's own TradingApp Store. Read full review

TD Ameritrade Best Desktop Platform

TD Ameritrade thinks or swim is our No. 1 desktop platform for 2020 and is home to an impressive array of tools. Highlights include virtual trading with fake money, performing advanced earnings analysis, plotting economic (FRED) data, charting social sentiment, backtesting, and even replaying historical markets tick-by-tick. TD Ameritrade also enables traders to create and conduct real-time stock scans, share charts and workspace layouts, and perform advanced options analysis. Read full review

Interactive Brokers Best For Professionals

As our top pick for professionals in 2020, the Interactive Brokers Trader Workstation (TWS) platform offers programmable hotkeys and a slew of order types for placing every possible trade imaginable, including algorithmic orders. Popular among the institutional community, including hedge funds, Interactive Brokers isn't beginner-friendly but does offer the lowest margin rates in the industry. Just beware, Interactive Brokers requires a $100,000 minimum deposit for margin accounts. Read full review

Fidelity Best Order Execution

Fidelity was ranked first overall for order execution, providing traders industry-leading order fills alongside a competitive platform. For day traders, Active Trader Pro (ATP) is Fidelity's flagship desktop platform and includes several unique, in-house brewed tools, including Real-Time Analytics (streaming trade signals) and Trade Armor (real-time position analysis). Read full review

E-TRADE Best Web-Based Platform

Built as a web-based platform, Power E*TRADE innovates and delivers speed, ease of use, and the tools needed for traders to succeed. Once again, in our 2020 Review, Power E*TRADE won our award, "Best Web-Based Platform." E*TRADE also took our top spot for options trading.

Day Trading Tools: Essential Tools For Success

Day trading requires that you have a set of tools and services to do your job effectively. Some of the required tools you likely already have. Modern-day trading is electronic, so day traders access the financial markets via the internet. It's also a good idea to have a telephone in case you need to call your broker, and you will need a computer or laptop to access the internet and make your trades.

Other tools you may not have yet. These include a direct access brokerage, real-time market data, and a trading-charting platform. All these tools and services are broken down in greater detail below, so you can see what you need, and get your day trading career started on the right path. Traders need many tools for their active trading lifestyle. These include the basics of hardware, software, and other more standard physical desk items.

Some tools are tangible. However, the more important ones are intangible and ever-evolving. Day trading is serious. The skill of day trading requires specific tools to generate the best outcomes. Some trading tools cost money. Others are free. Still, others need more time to forge. Consider trading as a business. In comparison to other businesses, overhead and variable costs are low. The costs are also predictable with proper planning. Ensure that you have these 17 essential tools to maximize your day trading success.

1. Computer Or Laptop For Day Trading

Technology is constantly changing, so make sure you have a computer with enough memory and a fast enough processor that it isn't constantly lagging, crashing or stalling (taking forever to load). Most trading and charting software require memory and processors that are fast and up to date. You may be jumping between company and broker websites and your charting software screens as you analyze a trade. Having two monitors is preferred, but not a necessity. One of the more contentious requirements in trading is the need for a fast computer. The availability of platforms that have mobile interface capabilities also fuels this debate.

However, the discussion ends when it comes to day trading. Those who are serious about results need to have a fast computer. Computers are an expense that only appears once every few years. Spend the money on a performance machine. The simplest guideline to follow is:

❖ If (video) gamers think it's a good computer, it will likely be great for day trading too. Don't let a slow computer bog down your trading efforts."

❖ High-performance laptops are an option for traders who need portability. The cost of this flexibility is a slight increase in price. Whatever computer you choose, make sure that it is never the factor holding back your trading.

2. Day Trading Charting Software

Most brokers (discussed below) provide several software options that traders can use to trade and monitor the price charts of financial assets. Day traders want to use trading software that allows them to easily pull up price charts, with an option to view tick charts and timed charts (1-minute, 5-minute, hourly, etc).

Different software is designed for different types of traders. Day traders need software that allows them to make trades quickly, without a lot of redundant or unnecessary steps. NinjaTrader is popular software that allows for trading and charting. Overall, the software can be utilized in multiple ways. Some software programs are compatible with certain brokerages. Some brokerages have software for all in one access. In some cases, you may have software add-ins that can connect with your trading systems in different ways to support your trading efforts. Finding the best software for your trading needs and connecting it with your trading service is important for the success of your trading activities.

3. Telephone

If your internet isn't available, you need a way to contact your broker other than email or online support. Have a landline, cell phone, or both available to you whenever you are trading. Have your broker's phone number programmed into your phone in case you need to call them. Remember, you may not be able to look up their number if you don't have internet access or your computer crashes.

4. Internet Access

Your internet should be fast enough that you can load web pages instantaneously. If it can't do that, your internet connection may be too slow for day trading. When you day trade thousands of data points are streaming to your computer each second, as asset prices move.

Your internet needs to keep up with that stream of constant data. If it can't (or if your computer is too slow to process the data), you will experience lag. Lag is when you are receiving old data instead of the newest data...basically, you have a data backlog and can't see current prices. Test out the different internet speeds offered by your internet service provider. Choose the one which provides fast webpage load-times and doesn't cause your trading software to lag.

5. Backup Internet Access

Services outages occasionally occur. Ideally, you want to be able to access your trading platform if an internet service outage occurs. A convenient way to do this is through a Smart Phone, which has internet access through a mobile data plan or hot spot. The plan should be provided by a different company than your internet service provider. That way, if your normal internet goes down, you can access the internet and your broker through your Smart Phone plan.

6. Day Trading Brokerage

To be a day trader you need a broker--a company that facilitates your trades. Not all brokers are created equal, and some cater to day traders more than others. Day traders make a lot of trades, which means they require a broker that provides low commissions as well as a trading software that works well for day trading. Major banks offer brokerage services, but typically their commissions are high and they don't offer customized solutions to day traders.

Therefore, smaller but regulated brokers are recommended for day traders. If you have trading software that you like to use, then search for brokers that allow their traders to use that software. That will narrow down the number of brokers you need to research and choose from. Different brokerages also have different access levels to markets. If you trade stocks, options, futures, or forex you may need to use different brokers.

7. Timely Market Data

Trading requires a constant stream of financial data, created by the movement of prices in the assets and markets you are trading. Your broker will provide you with market data, but you need to request the type of data you want. If you want to trade stocks, you need stock market data. You must specify if you want data for the NYSE or NASDAQ stock exchange, for example, if you want to see Level II data.

If you trade futures, you need to specify which contracts you are trading so you can see the pricing information for that specific contract. With many brokers you pay for stock and futures market data, so only subscribe to data you need. Some brokers give you all market data for free, but typically their commissions are higher in exchange. Forex brokers typically provide data for all forex pairs for free, so you just need to open a chart to see the price data.

8. Trading Plan

The most often overlooked aspect of day trading is the trading plan. It's an easy oversight to make. The best trading plans involve customization for the individual trader. This means they are not advertised on mass. Everyone wants to sell you a "one size fits all" strategy. But the generic plan is not the one that will get you where you want to go. What every trader needs to remember is that trading is a business. Businesses need plans for how they are going to succeed. Make sure you have a trading plan that at very least covers all the remaining points on this list.

9. Trading Platform

Many brokers offer their proprietary trading platform. A trading platform is a software used to enter orders. Many also let you analyze data to make trading decisions. In contrast, there are some excellent broker-independent or multi-broker trading platforms. These specialized tools allow trading at many brokerages through one software interface.

"A trading platform is to a trader as a cockpit is to a pilot."

The are several advantages of a multi-broker platform. They include not having to learn a new platform if your broker goes out of business. They are also helpful if you find your needs better served by a different brokerage and decide to switch. Broker independent multi-broker platforms also have a narrower focus. They are in the business of providing an excellent platform and concentrate on that.

10. Data Feed

Trading platforms need a data feed. Some trading platforms include the data feed for free, and others do not. Data comes in the form of historical and real-time trading prices and volumes as well as news feeds. My preferred data feed is Kinetick. It's designed to work with Ninjatrader and is fast and reliable. I use Kinetic data and don't plan on switching to another provider any time soon. Whichever data feed you choose, make sure it provides the right products and markets for you. You can pick and choose what you need, and set things up the way you like them.

11. Capital

"It takes money to make money."

There are many businesses where pure ingenuity and strategy are all that you need. Creativity makes the necessity for money a smaller concern. Day trading is not one of them. You might be a stock day trader meeting the pattern day trader requirements. Or you might be a futures trader meeting margin requirements. No matter what the situation, trading requires capital. Save money and make your trading path easier.

12. Education

Education and training is the only true secret weapon tool in the markets. Ignoring this tool is the underlying reason behind many trading failure stories. Doctors need education and training. Lawyers need education and training. Starbucks baristas need education and training. Despite these truths, many aspiring traders take the plunge unprepared. They jump into the competitive world of trading without formal education and training. There's a standard objection:

"Training and education are expensive, and I don't have the money."

Here's the truth...

You can't afford NOT to pay for training and education for your trading career. The lesson is always cheap.

Some education and training programs and courses are expensive. There's no arguing it. The expense is always minuscule compared to the losses they can save you from taking. Large losses almost always materialize through ignorance and inexperience. If you think you have money to trade, invest it wisely and deposit it into your brain first. Your future self with thanks you. So will your trading account.

13. Practice

Fantastic trading methodologies exist. One trader may consider a strategy to be fantastic. Another trader may find little value in the same strategy. Practice, practice, and practice some more to improve your trading fast. You will figure out fast what methods work for you (and which don't). Practice, practice, and practice some more to improve your trading fast. The only way to find out whether a strategy is right for you is to try it for yourself. Test the method. More important, test the strategy and method the way you like to trade. Don't be in a hurry to do something that isn't right for you. Start with a simulator to build your trading experience. Follow it up with the appropriate steps to move that strategy into live trading.

14. Strategy

The variety of trading strategies is as diverse as the traders who deploy them. Many traders end up struggling because the choice is overwhelming. They often change their strategy after a short time based on what they see on the horizon. They consider anything new as working better in comparison to their current strategy. This is a bad pattern. Stick to one or two good, solid strategies and give them time to work.

"Strategy is everything in trading."

Strategies take time to show consistent and favorable results. Start with fewer trading strategies so that you can excel at them free of distraction. Then add or subtract to your strategy list as your trading mastery and results dictate.

15. Specific Tools

Strategies within the day trading arena vary a lot. Even the tools to deploy the different strategies are quite specific.

For Example:

❖ High-quality news feeds benefit a strategy that trades breaking news and earnings releases. But the same news feed might be a waste of money for trader dealing with chart patterns.

❖ High precision historical databases and backtesting engines can be powerful. They are a fantastic asset to traders who use 100% automated systems. The same tools would be inappropriate for traders with a discretionary method.

❖ Proprietary indicators are a welcome expense for capable traders. These traders benefit and build a strong business case for the expense. The same indicators have less value to a trader who is unable to incorporate the tool into his trading plan.

Strengthen your trading operations. Ensure that you have the best tools, but only for the strategies that you trade. There is no need to own and use every tool out there. Successful traders specialize. This also means they chose specialized tools for their focus. Make sure you pick the arsenal of tools that fit your own strategies best.

16. Discipline

You will not find it on a store shelf. It is non-existent online. And it is not something with which any of us are born. Discipline. It's one of the most essential tools for successful trading.

"Nothing can stand in the way of true discipline." quote=" Nothing can stand in the way of true discipline."

Discipline in trading can come in the form of learning and practicing for the experience. It takes the form of setting aside as little as 30 minutes a day without fail. The hallmark of discipline is consistency. Doing the right thing over and over again without failing to show up and at least try is key. It's what needs to happen for trading success.

17. Commitment

Long term commitment can be elusive. Trading is a challenge, and true trading mastery takes years. A strong commitment is an intangible tool. It keeps traders sticking to their discipline over the long run. For the committed, there is always away. You can find the success you desire in the markets. Remember that overnight successes are rare. Long-lived overnight successes are nonexistent. Commit to trading. Whether the storms that will deliver you to the sunny beach of trading success.

The Best Day Trading Strategies

Your main goal as a day trader is to catch a potential daily trend and to exit at the right moment, which should happen before the end of the trading session. Notice that in some of the strategies, you'll also use a volume indicator to confirm our signals. Valid signals and trends are likely to occur during increasing or high trading volume.

Day trading is a trading style that involves opening and closing your trades intraday through margin accounts, which means you borrow extra funds from your day trading broker to trade with larger amounts of money. A day trading strategy involves a set of trading rules for opening and closing trading positions. There are many different trading strategies based on the indicators and the signals you use. Different indicator combinations give you different results.

Trading Strategies For Beginners

Before you get bogged down in a complex world of highly technical indicators, focus on the basics of a simple day trading strategy. Many make the mistake of thinking you need a highly complicated strategy to succeed intraday, but often the more straightforward, the more effective.

The Basics

Incorporate The Invaluable Elements Below Into Your Strategy.

1. **Money Management:** Before you start, sit down and decide how much you're willing to risk. Bear in mind most successful traders won't put more than 2% of their capital on the line per trade. You have to prepare yourself for some losses if you want to be around when the wins start rolling in.

2. **Time Management:** Don't expect to make a fortune if you only allocate an hour or two a day to trading. You need to constantly monitor the markets and be on the lookout for trade opportunities.

3. **Start Small:** Whilst you're finding your feet, stick to a maximum of three stocks during a single day. It's better to get good at a few than to be average and making no money on loads.

4. **Education:** Understanding market intricacies isn't enough, you also need to stay informed. Make sure you stay up to date with market news and any events that will impact your asset, such as a shift in economic policy. You can find a wealth of online financial and business resources that will keep you in the know.

5. **Consistency:** It's harder than it looks to keep emotions at bay when you're five coffees in and you've been staring at the screen for hours. You need to let maths, logic and your strategy guide you, not nerves, fear, or greed.

6. **Timing:** The market will get volatile when it opens each day and while experienced day traders may be able to read the patterns and profit, you should bide your time. So hold back for the first 15 minutes, you've still got hours ahead.

7. **Demo Account:** A must-have tool for any beginner, but also the best place to backtest or experiment with new, or

refined, strategies for advanced traders. Many demo accounts are unlimited, so not time-restricted.

Components Every Strategy Needs

Whether you're after automated day trading strategies, or beginner and advanced tactics, you'll need to take into account three essential components; volatility, liquidity, and volume. If you're to make money on tiny price movements, choosing the right stock is vital. These three elements will help you make that decision.

1. **Liquidity:** This enables you to swiftly enter and exit trades at an attractive and stable price. Liquid commodity strategies, for example, will focus on gold, crude oil, and natural gas.

2. **Volatility:** This tells you your potential profit range. The greater the volatility, the greater profit, or loss you may make. The cryptocurrency market is one such example well known for high volatility.

3. **Volume:** This measurement will tell you how many times the stock/asset has been traded within a set period. For day traders, this is better known as 'average daily trading volume.' High volume tells you there's a significant interest in the asset or security. An increase in volume is

frequently an indicator a price jump either up or down, is fast approaching.

What Makes Up A Good Day Trading Strategy

Indicators play a large role in strategy. Make sure you have the following.

1. Clear Trading Signals: Your trading strategy should involve clear rules for opening and closing your trades. The more they're based on technical criteria, the easier they'll be for you to implement. The fewer personal thoughts you involve, the less hesitation there will in your decision-making process.

2. Clear Stop-Loss Rules: Your trading strategy should involve good stop-loss rules. Always use a stop-loss on each of your trades, which limits your risk. It's always a good approach to risk no more than 1-2% of your bankroll in a single trade. You'll need 50-100 consecutive losing trades to lose all funds in your account. Imagine a coin-flipping 50-100 "heads" in a row. How likely is this to happen when you follow a strict trading strategy?

3. Success Rate: A good trading strategy will have a success rate relatively positive to the risk you take. It should give you higher returns than your losses in the long run. Notice that a strategy with a success rate lower than 50% can still be successful. Imagine that your strategy has a 40% success rate. This means that four out of 10 trades reach your preliminary set target. Now, imagine that your risk-to-return ratio is 1 to 10. This means that with risking one, you aim to get 10. In 40% of all cases, you'll be correct. This way, the 40% success rate strategy appears to be a great trading approach. Unfortunately, it's not that simple and will take hundreds of trades to determine the exact success rate and potential profit targets of your strategy.

Just remember, the higher your trading strategy's target, the lower your success rate will be. The results of your testing will strongly depend on your discipline during the trading process. One step outside of the rules will change your day trading strategy's potential.

Day Trading Strategies

Day trading strategies are essential when you are looking to capitalize on frequent, small price movements. A consistent, effective strategy relies on in-depth technical analysis, utilizing charts, indicators, and patterns to predict future price movements. This page will give you a thorough break down of beginners' trading strategies, working up to advanced, automated, and even asset-specific strategies. It will also outline some regional differences to be aware of, as well as pointing you in the direction of some useful resources. Ultimately though, you'll need to find a day trading strategy that suits your specific trading style and requirements.

1. Knowledge Is Power

In addition to knowledge of basic trading procedures, day traders need to keep up on the latest stock market news and events that affect stocks—the Fed's interest rate plans, the economic outlook, etc. So do your homework. Make a wish list of stocks you'd like to trade and keep yourself informed about the selected companies and general markets. Scan business news and visit reliable financial websites.

2. Set Aside Funds

Assess how much capital you're willing to risk on each trade. Many successful day traders risk less than 1% to 2% of their account per trade. If you have a $40,000 trading account and are willing to risk 0.5% of your capital on each trade, your maximum loss per trade is $200 (0.5% * $40,000). Set aside a surplus amount of funds you can trade with and you're prepared to lose. Remember, it may or may not happen.

3. Set Aside Time, Too

Day trading requires your time. That's why it's called day trading. You'll need to give up most of your day. Don't consider it if you have limited time to spare. The process requires a trader to track the markets and spot opportunities, which can arise at any time during trading hours. Moving quickly is key.

4. Start Small

As a beginner, focus on a maximum of one to two stocks during a session. Tracking and finding opportunities is easier with just a few stocks. Recently, it has become increasingly common to be able to trade fractional shares, so you can specify specific, smaller dollar amounts you wish to invest. That means if Apple shares are trading at $250 and you only want to buy $50 worth, many brokers will now let you purchase one-fifth of a share.

5. Avoid Penny Stocks

You're probably looking for deals and low prices but stay away from penny stocks. These stocks are often illiquid, and chances of hitting a jackpot are often bleak. Many stocks trading under $5 a share become de-listed from major stock exchanges and are only tradable over-the-counter (OTC). Unless you see a real opportunity and have done your research, stay clear of these.

6. Time Those Trades

Many orders placed by investors and traders begin to execute as soon as the markets open in the morning, which contributes to price volatility. A seasoned player may be able to recognize patterns and pick appropriately to make profits. But for newbies, it may be better just to read the market without making any moves for the first 15 to 20 minutes. The middle hours are usually less volatile, and then movement begins to pick up again toward the closing bell. Though the rush hours offer opportunities, it's safer for beginners to avoid them at first.

7. Cut Losses With Limit Orders

Decide what type of orders you'll use to enter and exit trades. Will you use market orders or limit orders? When you place a market order, it's executed at the best price available at the time thus, no price guarantee. A limit order, meanwhile, guarantees the price but not the execution. Limit orders help you trade with more precision, wherein you set your price (not unrealistic but executable) for buying as well as selling. More sophisticated and experienced day traders may employ the use of options strategies to hedge their positions as well.

8. Be Realistic About Profits

A strategy doesn't need to win all the time to be profitable. Many traders only win 50% to 60% of their trades. However, they make more on their winners than they lose on their losers. Make sure the risk on each trade is limited to a specific percentage of the account, and that entry and exit methods are clearly defined and written down.

9. Stay Cool

There are times when the stock markets test your nerves. As a day trader, you need to learn to keep greed, hope, and fear at bay. Decisions should be governed by logic and not emotion.

10. Stick To The Plan

Successful traders have to move fast, but they don't have to think fast. Why? Because they've developed a trading strategy in advance, along with the discipline to stick to that strategy. It is important to follow your formula closely rather than try to chase profits. Don't let your emotions get the best of you and abandon your strategy. There's a mantra among day traders: "Plan your trade and trade your plan."

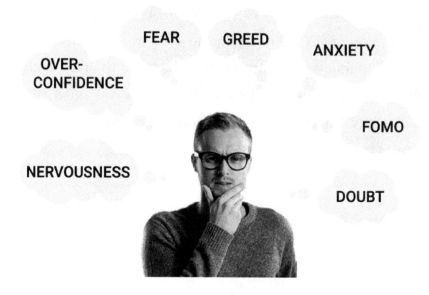

Trading Psychology: Beyond The Basics

The psychology of trading is often overlooked but forms a crucial part of a professional trader's skillset. I am the perfect place to learn how to manage your emotions and hone your trading psychology; mine analysts have already experienced the ups and downs, so you don't have to. Keep reading to discover their top tips, and to learn more about:

- ❖ What is trading psychology
- ❖ How to get in the mindset of a successful trader
- ❖ The basics of trading psychology
- ❖ The Importance of Trading Psychology

What is Trading Psychology?

Trading psychology refers to the emotions and mental state that help to dictate success or failure in trading securities. Trading psychology represents various aspects of an individual's character and behaviors that influence their trading actions. Trading psychology can be as important as other attributes such as knowledge, experience, and skill in determining trading success.

Discipline and risk-taking are two of the most critical aspects of trading psychology since a trader's implementation of these aspects are critical to the success of his or her trading plan. While fear and greed are the two most commonly known emotions associated with trading psychology, other emotions that drive trading behavior are hope and regret.

Trading psychology is a broad term that includes all the emotions and feelings that a typical trader will encounter when trading. Some of these emotions are helpful and should be embraced while others like fear, greed, nervousness, and anxiety should be contained. The psychology of trading is complex and takes time to fully master.

In reality, many traders experience the negative effects of trading psychology more than the positive aspects. Instances of this can appear in the form of closing losing trades prematurely, as the fear of loss gets too much or simply doubling down on losing positions when the fear of realizing a loss turns to greed.

One of the most treacherous emotions prevalent in financial markets is the fear of missing out or FOMO as it is known. Parabolic rises entice traders to buy after the movie has peaked, leading to huge emotional stress when the market reverses and moves in the opposite direction. Traders that manage to benefit from the positive aspects of psychology, while managing the bad aspects, are better placed to handle the volatility of the financial markets and become a better trader.

Understanding Trading Psychology

Trading psychology can be associated with a few specific emotions and behaviors that are often catalysts for market trading. Conventional characterizations of emotionally-driven behavior in markets ascribe most emotional trading to either greed or fear.

Greed can be thought of as an excessive desire for wealth, so excessive that it clouds rationality and judgment at times. Thus this characterization of greed-inspired investor or trading assumes that this emotion often leads traders towards a variety of behaviors. This may include making high-risk trades, buying shares of an untested company or technology just because it is going up in price rapidly, or buying shares without researching the underlying investment.

Additionally, greed may inspire investors to stay in profitable trades longer than is advisable to squeeze out extra profits from it, or to take on large speculative positions. Greed is most apparent in the final phase of bull markets when speculation runs rampant and investors throw caution to the wind.

Conversely, fear causes traders to close out positions prematurely or to refrain from taking on the risk because of concern about large losses. Fear is palpable during bear markets, and it is a potent emotion that can cause traders and investors to act irrationally in their haste to exit the market. Fear often morphs into a panic, which generally causes significant selloffs in the market from panic selling. Regret may cause a trader to get into a trade after initially missing out on it because the stock moved too fast. This is a violation of trading discipline and often results in indirect losses from security prices that are falling from peak highs.

The Basics Of Trading Psychology

Managing Emotions

Fear, greed, excitement, overconfidence, and nervousness are all typical emotions experienced by traders at some point or another. Managing the emotions of trading can prove to be the difference between growing the account equity or going bust.

Understanding FOMO

Traders need to identify and suppress FOMO as soon as it arises. While this isn't easy, traders should remember there will always be another trade and should only trade with the capital they can afford to lose.

Avoiding Trading Mistakes

While all traders make mistakes regardless of experience, understanding the logic behind these mistakes may limit the snowball effect of trading impediments. Some of the common trading mistakes include trading in numerous markets, inconsistent trading sizes, and overleveraging.

Overcoming Greed

Greed is one of the most common emotions among traders and therefore, deserves special attention. When greed overpowers logic, traders tend to double down on losing trades or use excessive leverage to recover previous losses. While it is easier said than done, traders must understand how to control greed when trading.

Importance Of Consistent Trading

New trades often tend to look for opportunities wherever they may appear and get lured into trading many different markets, with little or no regard for the inherent differences in these markets. Without a well thought out strategy that focuses on a handful of markets, traders can expect to see inconsistent results. Learn how to trade consistently.

"Trade according to your strategy, not your feelings" – Peter Hanks, Junior Analyst

Debunking Trading Myths

As individuals, we are often influenced by what we hear and trading is no different. There are many rumors around trading such as traders must have a large account to be successful, or that to be profitable, traders need to win most trades. These trading myths can often become a mental barrier, preventing individuals from trading.

Implementing Risk Management

The significance of effective risk management cannot be overstated. The psychological benefits of risk management are endless. Being able to define the target and stop-loss, upfront, allows traders to breathe a sigh of relief because they understand how much they are willing to risk in the pursuit of reaching the target. Another aspect of risk management involves position sizing and its psychological benefits:

"One of the easiest ways to decrease the emotional effect of your trades is to lower your trade size" – James Stanley, DFX Currency Strategist

How To Get In The Mindset Of A Successful Trader

While many nuances contribute to the success of professional traders, there are a few common approaches that traders of all levels can consistently implement within their particular trading strategy.

1. Bring A Positive Attitude To The Markets Every Day: This may seem obvious, but in reality, keeping a positive attitude when speculating in the forex market is difficult, especially after a run of successive losses. A positive attitude will keep your mind clear of negative thoughts that tend to get in the way of placing new trades.

2. Put Aside Your Ego: Accept that you are going to get trades wrong and that you may even lose more trades than you win. This may seem like all bad news but with discipline and prudent risk management, it is still possible to grow account equity by ensuring average winners outweigh the average losses.

3. Do Not Trade For The Sake Of Trading: You can only take what the market gives you. Some days you may place fifteen trades and in other instances, you may not place a single trade for two weeks. It all depends on what is happening in the market and whether trade setups - that align with your strategy - appear in the market.

"Trade decisions are not binary, long vs short. Sometimes doing nothing is the best trade you can make" – Ilya Spivak, Senior Currency Strategist

4. Do Not Get Despondent: This may seem similar to the first point but deals with thoughts of quitting. Many people see trading as a get rich quick scheme when in fact, it is more of a journey of trade after trade. This expectation of instant gratification often leads to frustration and impatience. Remember to stay disciplined and stay the course and view trading as a journey.

Technical Analysis

Trading psychology is often important for technical analysts relying on charting techniques to drive their trade decisions. Security charting can provide a broad array of insights on a security's movement. While technical analysis and charting techniques can be helpful in spotting trends for buying and selling opportunities, it requires an understanding and intuition for market movements which is derived from an investor's trading psychology.

There are numerous instances in technical charting where a trader must rely not only on the chart's insight but also on their knowledge of the security that they're following and their intuition for how broader factors are affecting the market. Traders with keen attention to comprehensive security price influences, discipline, and confidence show balanced trading psychology that typically contributes to profitable success.

Key Takeaways

* ❖ Trading psychology is the emotional component of an investor's decision-making process which may help explain why some decisions appear more rational than others.
* ❖ Trading psychology is characterized primarily as the influence of both greed and fear.
* ❖ Greed drives decisions that appear to accept too much risk.
* ❖ Fear drives decisions that appear to avoid risk and generate too little return.

The Importance of Trading Psychology

Many skills are required for trading successfully in the financial markets. They include the abilities to evaluate a company's fundamentals and to determine the direction of a stock's trend. But neither of these technical skills is as important as the trader's mindset.

Containing emotion, thinking quickly, and exercising discipline are components of what we might call trading psychology. There are two main emotions to understand and keep under control: fear and greed.

1. Snap Decisions

Traders often have to think fast and make quick decisions, darting in and out of stocks on short notice. To accomplish this, they need a certain presence of mind. They also need the discipline to stick with their trading plans and know when to book profits and losses. Emotions simply can't get in the way.

2. Understanding Fear

When traders get bad news about a certain stock or the economy in general, they naturally get scared. They may overreact and feel compelled to liquidate their holdings and sit on the cash, refraining from taking any more risks. If they do, they may avoid certain losses but may also miss out on some gains.

Traders need to understand what fear is: a natural reaction to a perceived threat. In this case, it's a threat to their profit potential. Quantifying the fear might help. Traders should consider just what they are afraid of, and why they are afraid of it. But that thinking should occur before the bad news, not in the middle of it.

By thinking it through ahead of time, traders will know how they perceive events instinctively and react to them and can move past the emotional response. Of course, this is not easy, but it's necessary for the health of an investor's portfolio, not to mention the investor.

3. Overcoming Greed

There's an old saying on Wall Street that "pigs get slaughtered." This refers to the habit greedy investors have of hanging on to a winning position too long to get every last tick upward in price. Sooner or later, the trend reverses and the greedy get caught.

Greed is not easy to overcome. It's often based on the instinct to do better, to get just a little more. A trader should learn to recognize this instinct and develop a trading plan based on rational thinking, not whims or instincts.

4. Setting Rules

A trader needs to create rules and follow them when the psychological crunch comes. Set out guidelines based on your risk-reward tolerance for when to enter a trade and when to exit it. Set a profit target and put a stop loss in place to take emotion out of the process.

Besides, you might decide which specific events, such as a positive or negative earnings release, should trigger a decision to buy or sell a stock. It's wise to set limits on the maximum amount you are willing to win or lose in a day. If you hit the profit target, take the money and run. If your losses hit a predetermined number, fold up your tent and go home.

5. Conducting Research And Review

Traders need to become experts in the stocks and industries that interest them. Keep on top of the news, educate yourself and, if possible, go to trading seminars and attend conferences. Devote as much time as possible to the research process. That means studying charts, speaking with management, reading trade journals, and doing other background work such as macroeconomic analysis or industry analysis.

"Knowledge can also help overcome fear".

Stay Flexible

Traders need to remain flexible and consider experimenting from time to time. For example, you might consider using options to mitigate risk. One of the best ways a trader can learn is by experimenting (within reason). The experience may also help reduce emotional influences.

Finally, traders should periodically assess their performances. In addition to reviewing their returns and individual positions, traders should reflect on how they prepared for a trading session, how up to date they are on the markets, and how they're progressing in terms of ongoing education. This periodic assessment can help a trader correct mistakes, change bad habits, and enhance overall returns.

CHAPTER 8 - STEP BY STEP TO A SUCCESSFUL TRADE

Day Trading For Beginners: A Step-By-Step Guide

Day trading is an approach to the marketplace in which a trader buys and sells a futures contract within the same session. Traders manage open positions within the constraints of an intraday methodology, with no open positions held at the daily closing bell. Day trading strategies commonly target futures, forex, and stocks. The discipline of day trading is controversial. Industry traditionalists argue that short-term trading resembles gambling more than it does invest. Proponents argue that although day trading for beginners may be a challenge, it's feasible and potentially very lucrative. Either way, no shortage of traders engage the markets exclusively via day trading strategies.

However, before embarking on the journey from novice to seasoned market veteran, beginners should take a few basic steps at the outset.

Step One: Self-Assessment

Before starting any new endeavor, it's always a good idea to take a long look in the mirror and ask the tough questions. Because the modern marketplace is a fast-moving, hypercompetitive atmosphere, a period of introspection before entering can be extremely useful in overcoming challenges as they arise. Conducting a rugged self-assessment is an important initial step in developing into a competent day trader. A self-assessment should include the following elements:

1. Personality Type: A simple personality test can help shed some light on your psychological makeup. Personal characteristics such as being a risk-taker or being prone to impulsive behavior can impact performance dramatically.

2. Goals: Understanding what your goals and objectives are before active trading begins is critical to finding a sustainable trading niche in the markets.

3. Attributes: Having a grasp on key personal strengths and weaknesses is a big part of identifying areas that need improvement. If you're not technologically savvy or are terrible with numbers, then shoring up these areas can help improve your market experience.

Day trading is not for everyone. Understanding your potential compatibility with the trading environment as a whole is a great way to save time and money before placing your first trade.

Step Two: Acquire The Necessary Components

Over the past several decades, the ranks of active traders have grown dramatically. Advances in online technologies have lowered many of the traditional barriers to entry, bringing the markets to the masses. The contemporary marketplace is an almost exclusively digital venue. To interact with it competently, there are three necessary components:

1. **Hardware:** Whether it's a desktop or mobile device, basic computing power is a necessity.

2. **Market Connectivity:** Securing a functional internet connection is a prerequisite for accessing brokerage and exchange servers.

3. **Software Trading Platform:** The platform is the trader's portal to the marketplace. Analyzing streaming data and placing market orders in real-time is best facilitated via a robust software suite.

It's never been easier to become involved in the financial markets. Regardless of your time zone, capital resources, or level of experience, pursuing your market-related goals is now possible.

Step Three: Building A Plan

No primer on day trading for beginners is complete without addressing the need for a comprehensive plan. The most important part of day trading is decision-making. Crafting sound decisions related to when, what, and how to trade efficiently are critical to the eventual success of the operation as a whole. A complete trading plan must include provisions for the following:

1. **Market Entry/Exit:** Identifying opportunity on-the-fly is a critical part of any trading strategy. A rules-based approach can streamline the process, ensuring optimal market entry and exit.

2. **Position Management:** A structured plan can clearly define the location of stop losses and profit targets on a per-trade basis. Advanced systems may include scaling, break-even, and trailing stop functionality.

3. **Risk Management:** Getting the most out of your risk capital is an integral part of day trading. Knowing your exposure within the context of a viable risk vs. reward scenario is the key to not becoming overextended.

A comprehensive strategy ensures that trade-related actions are carried out in a consistent and disciplined manner. Without a strategy, results are not quantifiable and profit or loss often resembles wild luck. Day trading can be financially rewarding, yet challenging, endeavor. Nonetheless, given the proper due diligence, engaging the markets successfully is possible.

Steps To Becoming A Day Trader

In a world where everyone has easy access to online trading, why are there only a few succeeding as day traders? After all, what investor has not dreamed of becoming a day trader working comfortably at a home computer, being your boss, watching profits roll in? While many aspire, few succeed.

What Does A Day Trader Do?

A day trader actively buys and sells securities, often multiple times during the day, but without carrying any open positions to the next day. All buy/sell positions taken during a trading day are squared-off on the same day before the market closes. Day traders are different from active traders who may hold a position for multiple days, or from investors who invest for longer periods. Day traders also use leverage to increase their intraday trade exposure.

How To Become A Day Trader

1. Conduct A Self-Assessment

Successful day trading requires a combination of knowledge, skills, and traits as well as a commitment to a lifestyle. Are you adept with mathematical analysis, full of financial knowledge, aware of behavioral psychology (in yourself as well as others), and do you have the stomach for entrepreneurship? Contrary to the perceived notion of an easy life or easy money, day trading requires:

- ❖ Long working hours
- ❖ Very little leave from work
- ❖ Continuous self-learning with no guidance
- ❖ Risk-taking abilities
- ❖ Never-ending commitment to daily activities of the job

The right mindset is the most important (and the very first) requirement in becoming a day trader. Unless one is prepared to devote time, self-learn, and be mentally prepared to take risks and suffer losses, do not try day trading. Books like Trade Your Way to Financial Freedom by Van Tharp and The Psychology of Trading by Brett N. Steenbarger are good resources for learning more about day trading and performing a self-assessment.

2. Arrange Sufficient Capital

No one can generate profits consistently. Intermittent and extended losses are part of the day trading game. (For example, a day trader may suffer eight loss-making trades in a row and only recover with profit on the ninth trade.)

To handle these risks, a day trader must have a sufficient cushion of capital. As Van Tharp explained in Trade Your Way to Financial Freedom, entering the trading world with only a small amount of money is a sure path to failure. Before quitting your job to trade full time, Tharp recommends having at least $100,000 for trading. Novices can start with smaller amounts, depending upon their selected trading plan, the frequency of trading, and other costs they bear. To actively day trade it is required that you maintain a balance of $10,000 in your trading account.

3. Understand The Markets

Day traders need a solid foundation of knowledge about how the markets function. From simple details (like exchange trading hours and holidays) to complex details (like the impact of news events, margin requirements, and allowed tradable instruments), a trader needs to have a broad knowledge base.

4. Understand Securities

Stocks, futures, options, ETFs, and mutual funds all trade differently. Without a clear understanding of a security's characteristics and trading requirements, initiating a trading strategy can lead to failure. For example, traders should know how margin requirements for futures, options, and commodities significantly impact trading capital or how an interim assignment or exercise of an option position can shatter the trading plan completely.

Lack of knowledge about these necessities specific to securities can lead to losses. Aspiring traders should ensure full familiarity with the trading of selected securities.

5. Setup A Trading Strategy

Novice traders entering the world of trading can begin by selecting at least two established trade strategies. Both would act as a backup of each other in case of failure or a lack of trading opportunities. One can move on to more number of strategies (with more complexities) later, as the experience builds up. The trading world is highly dynamic. Trading strategies can consistently make money for long periods but then fail at any time. One needs to keep a close eye on the effectiveness of the selected trading strategy and adapt, customize, dump, or substitute it depending upon the developments.

6. Integrate Strategy And Plan

Selecting the right trading strategies alone is not sufficient to succeed in the market. The following considerations need to complement the strategy, to come up with the trading plan:

- ❖ How the strategy will be used (entry/exit strategy)
- ❖ How much capital will be used
- ❖ How much money per trade will be used
- ❖ Which assets will be traded
- ❖ How frequency to place trades

7. Practice Money Management

Let's say you have $100,000 as trading capital and an excellent trading strategy that offers a 70% success rate (seven trades out of 10 are profitable). How much should you spend on your first trade? What if the first three trades are a failure? What if the average record (seven profitable trades out of 10) no longer holds? Or, while trading futures (or options), how should you allocate your capital to margin money requirements?

Money management helps you address these challenges and estimate your potential profitability. Effective money management can help you win even if there are only four profitable trades out of 10. Practice, plan and structure the trades according to money management and capital allocation plan.

8. Research Brokerage Charges

Day trading usually involves frequent transactions, which result in high brokerage costs. After thorough research, select the brokerage plan wisely. If one intends to play with one-two trades per day, then a per trade basis brokerage plan would be appropriate. If the daily trading volume is high, go for staggered plans (the higher the volume, the lower the effective cost) or fixed plans (unlimited trades for a fixed high charge)

Apart from trade execution, a broker also offers other trading utilities, which includes trading platforms, integrated trading solutions like option combinations, trading software, historical data, research tools, trading alerts, charting application with technical indicators and several other features. Some features may be free while some may come at a cost that can eat into your profits. It is advisable to select the features depending upon your trading needs and avoid subscribing to ones that are not needed. Novices should start with the low-cost basic brokerage package matching their initial trading needs and later opt for upgrades to other modules when needed.

9. Simulate And Back Test

Once the plan is ready, simulate it on a test account with virtual money (most brokers offer such test accounts). Alternatively, one can backtest the strategy on historical data. For a realistic assessment, keep consideration for brokerage costs and the subscription fee for various utilities.

10. Start Small And Then Expand

Even if you have sufficient money and sufficient experience, don't play big on the first trades of a new strategy. Try out a new strategy with a smaller amount and increase the stakes after tasting success. Remember, markets and trading opportunities will remain forever, but money, once lost, may be difficult to re-accumulate. Start small, test to establish, and then go for the big ones.

Steps To Building A Winning Trading Plan

There is an old expression in business that, if you fail to plan, you plan to fail. It may sound glib, but people that are serious about being successful, including traders, should follow those words as if they are written in stone. Ask any trader who makes money consistently and they will probably tell you that you have two choices:

❖ Methodically follow a written plan

❖ Fail.

If you already have a written trading or investment plan, congratulations, you are in the minority. It takes time, effort, and research to develop an approach or methodology that works in financial markets. While there are never any guarantees of success, you have eliminated one major roadblock by creating a detailed trading plan. If your plan uses flawed techniques or lacks preparation, your success won't come immediately, but at least you are in a position to chart and modify your course. By documenting the process, you learn what works and how to avoid the costly mistakes that newbie traders sometimes face. Whether or not you have a plan now, here are some ideas to help with the process.

Trading is a business, so you have to treat it as such if you want to succeed. Reading a few books, buying a charting program, opening a brokerage account, and starting to trade with real money is not a business plan, it is more like a recipe for disaster. A plan should be written, with clear signals that are not subject to change, while you are trading, but subject to reevaluation when the markets are closed. The plan can change with market conditions and might see adjustments as the trader's skill level improves. Each trader should write their plan, taking into account personal trading styles and goals. Using someone else's plan does not reflect your trading characteristics.

Building The Perfect Master Plan

No two trading plans are the same because no two traders are exactly alike. Each approach will reflect important factors like the trading style as well as risk tolerance. What are the other essential components of a solid trading plan? Here are 10 that every plan should include:

1. Skill Assessment

Are you ready to trade? Have you tested your system by paper trading it, and do you have confidence that it will work in a live trading environment? Can you follow your signals without hesitation? Trading the markets is a battle of giving and take. The real pros are prepared and take profits from the rest of the crowd who, lacking a plan, generally give money away after costly mistakes.

2. Mental Preparation

How do you feel? Did you get enough sleep? Do you feel up to the challenge ahead? If you are not emotionally and psychologically ready to do battle in the market, take the day off—otherwise, you risk losing your shirt. This is almost guaranteed to happen if you are angry, preoccupied, or otherwise distracted from the task at hand.

Many traders have a market mantra they repeat before the day begins to get them ready. Create one that puts you in the trading zone. Additionally, your trading area should be free of distractions. Remember, this is a business and distractions can be costly.

3. Set Risk Level

How much of your portfolio should you risk on one trade? This will depend on your trading style and tolerance for risk. The amount of risk can vary, but should probably range from around 1% to 5% of your portfolio on a given trading day. That means if you lose that amount at any point in the day, you get out of the market and stay out. It's better to take a break, and then fight another day if things aren't going your way.

4. Set Goals

Before you enter a trade, set realistic profit targets and risk/reward ratios. What is the minimum risk/reward you will accept? Many traders will not take a trade unless the potential profit is at least three times greater than the risk. For example, if your stop-loss is $1 per share, your goal should be a $3 per share in profit. Set weekly, monthly, and annual profit goals in dollars or as a percentage of your portfolio, and reassess them regularly.

5. Do Your Homework

Before the market opens, do you check what is going on around the world? Are overseas markets up or down? Are S&P 500 index futures up or down in the pre-market? Index futures are a good way of gauging the mood before the market opens because futures contracts trade day and night.

What are the economic or earnings data that are due out and when? Post a list on the wall in front of you and decide whether you want to trade ahead of an important report. For most traders, it is better to wait until the report is released rather than taking unnecessary risks associated with trading during the volatile reactions to reports. Pros trade based on probabilities. They don't gamble. Trading ahead of an important report is often a gamble because it is impossible to know how markets will react.

6. Trade Preparation

Whatever trading system and program you use, label major and minor support and resistance levels on the charts, set alerts for entry and exit signals, and make sure all signals can be easily seen or detected with a clear visual or auditory signal.

7. Set Exit Rules

Most traders make the mistake of concentrating most of their efforts on looking for buy signals, but pay very little attention to when and where to exit. Many traders cannot sell if they are down because they don't want to take a loss. Get over it, learn to accept losses, or you will not make it as a trader. If your stop gets hit, it means you were wrong. Don't take it personally. Professional traders lose more trades than they win, but by managing money and limiting losses, they still make profits.

Before you enter a trade, you should know your exits. There are at least two possible exits for every trade. First, what is your stop loss if the trade goes against you? It must be written down. Mental stops don't count. Second, each trade should have a profit target. Once you get there, sell a portion of your position and you can move your stop loss on the rest of your position to the breakeven point if you wish.

8. Set Entry Rules

This comes after the tips for exit rules for a reason: Exits are far more important than entries. A typical entry rule could be worded like this: "If signal A fires and there is a minimum target at least three times as great as my stop loss and we are at support, then buy X contracts or shares here."

Your system should be complicated enough to be effective, but simple enough to facilitate snap decisions. If you have 20 conditions that must be met and many are subjective, you will find it difficult (if not impossible) to make trades. Computers often make better traders than people, which may explain why nearly 50% of all trades that now occur on the New York Stock Exchange are generated by computer programs.

Computers don't have to think or feel good to make a trade. If conditions are met, they enter. When the trade goes the wrong way or hits a profit target, they exit. They don't get angry at the market or feel invincible after making a few good trades. Each decision is based on probabilities, not emotion.

9. Keep Excellent Records

Many experienced and successful traders are also excellent at keeping records. If they win a trade, they want to know exactly why and how. More importantly, they want to know the same when they lose, so they don't repeat unnecessary mistakes. Write down details such as targets, the entry and exit of each trade, the time, support and resistance levels, daily opening range, market open and close for the day, and record comments about why you made the trade as well as the lessons learned.

You should also save your trading records so that you can go back and analyze the profit or loss for a particular system, drawdowns (which are amounts lost per trade using a trading system), average time per trade (which is necessary to calculate trade efficiency), and other important factors. Also, compare these factors to a buy-and-hold strategy. Remember, this is a business and you are the accountant. You want your business to be as successful and profitable as possible.

10. Analyze Performance

After each trading day, adding up the profit or loss is secondary to knowing the why and how. Write down your conclusions in your trading journal so you can reference them later. Remember, there will always be losing trades. What you want is a trading plan that wins over the longer term.

To Ensure That You Get The Best Out Of This Guide, Keep In Mind The Rules Of Day Trading Listed Below:

Rule 1: Be aware of your market. Try to specialize and concentrate on a few selected markets or financial instruments. Over time, you will be attuned to the market or instruments that you have selected to focus on. In a way, you will develop a sixth sense of your market conditions.

Rule 2: Preparation is the key. Always prepare yourself properly before the next day's trading. You still need to do the necessary groundwork. In a way, this is like giving yourself a briefing about how, where, and when you will execute your trading strategy. Having an idea where to place your stop loss will ensure that you cover your loss point for the day. Thus, you can spend the major part of the day trading for profit.

Rule 3: Ensure that you stick to your trading plan. This will require immense discipline on your part but is an essential part of being a successful day trader.

Rule 4: Like rule 3, controlling your greed is not easy. This requires a high degree of self-control. Don't try to maximize every single point of your trade. At times, it is wiser to let go. In a fast-moving market, a winning trade can easily turn into a loss.

Rule 5: Sometimes you have to cut a losing position and when that time comes, you should not hesitate. It is better to take several small losses than wait for a big loss to come hit you and wipe out all your capital.

Rule 6: It is also important that you never try to catch the market. If for any reason, you miss out on a good trade because you were slow, do not decide to jump in at the later stage. It is likely that by the time you have entered the market, you will be doing so at the top end or low end of the deal. Skip the trade and return to trade the next day.

Rule 7: Never enter into a trade unless you have faith in what you are doing. Do not trade just for the sake of trading or because you are looking for excitement. In other words, do not overtrade.

Rule 8: Always trade with the trend. Never trade at the top or bottom end of the trend. The market is always fluid and it can go higher or lower than expected. If you stray from the trend range, you might find yourself on the wrong side of the trend.

Rule 9: Protecting your capital should always be your number one priority. Profitability is secondary. Controlling your losses will help ensure that you will live to trade another day. If you keep chasing profits and the market backtracks suddenly, you might find that a high proportion of your capital will be at risk.

Rule 10: Take note of upcoming news announcements. It is especially a bad idea to hold an open position before the announcement of any news which might move the market. Unless you can second-guess the market, you will never know what direction the market will move upon the announcement of the news.

CONCLUSION

Day trading requires time, skill, and discipline. Skill is developed over some time as you participate in the markets and trade with discipline by devoting your time. A sound understanding of some good day trading strategies can provide a foundation for this endeavor. Self-learning is the best way to learn, and as Jesse Livermore, a legendary trader said, "I know from experience that nobody can give me a tip or a series of tips that will make more money for me than my judgment."

Although day trading has become somewhat of a controversial phenomenon, it can be a viable way to earn a profit. Day traders, both institutional and individual, play an important role in the marketplace by keeping the markets efficient and liquid. While popular among inexperienced traders, it should be left primarily to those with the skills and resources needed to succeed

Day traders are active traders who execute intraday strategies to profit off-price changes for a given asset. Day trading employs a wide variety of techniques and strategies to capitalize on perceived market inefficiencies. Day trading is often characterized by technical analysis and requires a high degree of self-discipline and objectivity.

Day trading rules may be different for each trader, but controlling emotion and limiting losses is necessary for any strategy.

Beginning traders should trade accounts with "paper money," or fake trades before they invest their capital. Traders need a clear strategy before they begin trading. However, adjusting a strategy as time goes on and the trader becomes more aware of the market is equally as important.

Day trading and swing trading each have advantages and drawbacks. Neither strategy is better than the other, and traders should choose the approach that works best for their skills, preferences, and lifestyle. Day trading is better suited for individuals who are passionate about trading full time and possess the three Ds: decisiveness, discipline, and diligence (prerequisites for successful day trading).

Day trading success also requires an advanced understanding of technical trading and charting. Since day trading is intense and stressful, traders should be able to stay calm and control their emotions under fire. Finally, day trading involves risk—traders should be prepared to sometimes walk away with 100 percent losses.

There are endless horizons to explore with trading using computer programs and automated software systems. It may be extremely exciting to make money at the click of a button, but one needs to be fully aware of what's going behind the scenes: Is the automated order is getting at the right price in the right market, is it following the right strategy and so on. A lot of trading anomalies have been attributed to automated trading systems. A thorough evaluation of day-trading software with a clear understanding of your desired trading strategy can allow individual traders to reap the benefits of automated day trading.

Day trading is difficult to master. It requires time, skill, and discipline. Many of those who try it fail, but the techniques and guidelines described above can help you create a profitable strategy. With enough practice and consistent performance evaluation, you can greatly improve your chances of beating the odds

CPSIA information can be obtained
at www.ICGtesting.com
Printed in the USA
LVHW011703220221
679517LV00004B/175